GARY MILLAR

2 CORINTHIANS

FOR YOU

To my parents, John and Lorna (d 2002)
and my in-laws, Warner and Sheena,
With deep thankfulness in Christ for their relentless
love, support and encouragement

2 Corinthians For You

© Gary Millar, 2020.

Published by:
The Good Book Company

thegoodbook.com | www.thegoodbook.co.uk
thegoodbook.com.au | thegoodbook.co.nz | thegoodbook.co.in

A CIP record of this book is available from the British Library.

(Hardcover) ISBN: 9781784984090
(Paperback) ISBN: 9781784984106

Printed in India

Design by André Parker

CONTENTS

SERIES PREFACE

Each volume of the *God's Word For You* series takes you to the heart of a book of the Bible, and applies its truths to your heart.

The central aim of each title is to be:

- Bible centred
- Christ glorifying
- Relevantly applied
- Easily readable

You can use *2 Corinthians For You:*

To read. You can simply read from cover to cover, as a book that explains and explores the themes, encouragements and challenges of this part of Scripture.

To feed. You can work through this book as part of your own personal regular devotions, or use it alongside a sermon or Bible-study series at your church. Each chapter is divided into two (or occasionally three) shorter sections, with questions for reflection at the end of each.

To lead. You can use this as a resource to help you teach God's word to others, both in small-group and whole-church settings. You'll find tricky verses or concepts explained using ordinary language, and helpful themes and illustrations along with suggested applications.

These books are not commentaries. They assume no understanding of the original Bible languages, nor a high level of biblical knowledge. Verse references are marked in **bold** so that you can refer to them easily. Any words that are used rarely or differently in everyday language outside the church are marked in grey when they first appear, and are explained in a glossary towards the back. There, you'll also find details of resources you can use alongside this one, in both personal and church life.

Our prayer is that as you read, you'll be struck not by the contents of this book, but by the book it's helping you open up; and that you'll praise not the author of this book, but the One he is pointing you to.

Carl Laferton, Series Editor

Bible translations used:

■ ESV: English Standard Version (this is the version being quoted unless otherwise stated)

■ NIV: New International Version, 2011 edition

■ KJV: King James Version (also known as the Authorised Version)

INTRODUCTION TO 2 CORINTHIANS

After many years of passing through Changi Airport, I finally made it out through arrivals to actually spend some time in Singapore. And I loved it! Not only is chilli crab possibly the greatest dish under heaven, but the city is just about the most vibrant and complex place I have ever visited.

It's so British, with stunning colonial architecture.

It's so Asian, with hawker centres everywhere.

It's so American, with the soaring towers of the banking district dwarfing everything else.

It's so Chinese, with the island state's symbol—the "merlion"(a lion's head with a fish's tail)—standing proudly at the heart of the city.

Singapore, with its fusion of east and west, old and new, rich and poor, is just about as close to Corinth as we are ever likely to get.

Reinvented

Like Singapore, the port city of Corinth had an ancient history, but had recently been reinvented, refounded by **Julius Caesar*** in around 44 BC.

Like Singapore, Corinth rapidly became a flourishing financial and trade centre—by the middle of the first century it was booming.

Like Singapore, Corinth was a city where the pressure was on to climb the social and economic ladder—although such is the pressure on education that I think people from Singapore get higher grades.

Like Singapore, Corinth was a melting pot—it became home for a generation of Roman freedmen and retired soldiers, as well as many Jews who had been expelled from Rome by **Claudius** in AD 49. This group of Jewish exiles, alongside the native Greeks, threw themselves into life in this brash new city.

---

* Words in **grey** are defined in the Glossary (page 189).

When Paul showed up in Corinth for the first time, he found *a city with a Roman face, a Greek heart, a large Jewish minority and a deeply ingrained universal desire to impress.* It's hardly a shock then that when Paul preached the gospel and a church was born, life got pretty complicated. What else would you expect from a bunch of people who are mostly Greek, following a suffering and dying Jewish Messiah, in the middle of a Roman city which prides itself on always coming out on top. Welcome to the mess that is Corinth.

Now I know that church is always messy. I know that ministry is always more complicated than we first think. But it's also true that some places are more messy than others. And Corinth was one of those places. And Paul's relationship with the messy church he had planted in this complex city was—yes, you guessed it—*messy.*

Planting problems

After his initial stay in Corinth, when the church was planted (Acts 18:1-18), Paul heard that things had very quickly gone downhill. So about a year later, while he was in Ephesus, he wrote them a letter (now lost) explaining to them that sexual immorality in the church is not acceptable (he refers to that letter in 1 Corinthians 5:9).

That initial letter didn't do the trick, so about a year later (probably AD 53), he wrote the long letter that we know as 1 Corinthians, which covers a huge number of practical and theological issues.

You would hope that this might have fixed things in Corinth, but six months after that, Paul's apprentice, Timothy, passed through the port city and found that the church was in a complete mess. In fact, it was in *such* a mess that Paul dropped everything and made what he refers to in 2 Corinthians 2:1 as "the painful visit". Things did not go well, and it seems that Paul left Corinth unsure of whether the church would ever get back on track. His relationship with them was close to breaking point, and their grip on the gospel was weakening.

So he sent Titus with the letter he describes in 2:4:

"For I wrote to you out of much affliction and anguish of heart and with many tears, not to cause you pain but to let you know the abundant love that I have for you."

This letter seems to have had some positive effect, and so several months after that, sometime in late 54 or 55, two years after the church plant began and about a year after writing 1 Corinthians, Paul wrote 2 Corinthians (which confusingly was actually at least the fourth letter he'd written to them), which Titus again delivered.

It's important for us to appreciate this difficult history as we start to read 2 Corinthians because it goes some way to explaining why Paul both *loved* the Corinthians and was *driven nuts* by them in equal measure. He has more recorded interaction with them than any other church he planted. Their issues take up more of the New Testament than those of any other church. And at this point in their relationship, it was still not entirely clear whether the church would flourish and grow or crash and burn—which explains why this is the most passionate, honest, vulnerable, heartfelt letter in the Bible. The battle for hearts and minds was still on in Corinth. In particular, the leaders that Paul left behind continued to waver. So Paul wrote again in an attempt to persuade them to stick with him and the gospel.

> This letter is the place to go for a description and embodiment of what gospel ministry is all about.

That's why I think this letter is the place to go in the New Testament for a description and embodiment of what *gospel* ministry is all about. For Paul, "gospel ministry" is what we all do—it means walking with and serving Jesus. This letter is written *for all of us.*

Ministering with messy people

When it comes to ministry in the messiness of the church and the complexity of our world, I think this letter is the place to start. When it comes to Christian leadership, this letter is the place to start. When it comes to the battle for a gospel-shaped approach to life in our hearts and our minds, this is the place to start. When it comes to life in the mess, this is the place to start. 2 Corinthians walks us through how to live by faith in our broken world. It's the key to embracing our weakness and living in the strength which God himself supplies.

So let's get reading!

1. BEGINNING WITH GOD

As he writes another letter to his much-loved but thoroughly infuriating brothers and sisters in Corinth, in the first 11 verses Paul wants to make sure that whatever they are going through, whatever their issues may be, they have got the fact that God himself is the foundation of life and ministry. In this passage, Paul sets out a vision which is radically God-centred and rests on three huge convictions about God himself.

God rules and provides for his church

When writing a letter in the ancient world, the writer would start by introducing themselves. But Paul is never content simply to write his name; he always wants to pack as much encouragement and **theology** into his letters as possible—and 2 Corinthians is no exception. He starts like this:

> "Paul, an **apostle** of Christ Jesus by the will of God, … To the church of God that is at Corinth … **Grace** to you and peace from God our Father and the Lord Jesus Christ." (**1:1**)*

At the risk of stating the obvious, *this letter starts with God*.

Undergirding everything that Paul writes in this letter is the fact that *God rules and provides for his church*. The church is not *our* project; it is God's. The church is not *our* community; it is *God's*. Ultimately the church is not even *our* responsibility; it is *God's*. And when

---

* All 2 Corinthians verse references being looked at in each chapter part are in **bold**.

it comes to thinking about ministry, the Christian life and the church, this perspective changes everything.

Paul clearly sees himself as God's emissary, with the dignity and sense of responsibility which that brings. He says he is "an apostle of Christ Jesus by the will of God" (v 1). He doesn't come on his own authority, nor is he pursuing his own agenda. The idea of an "apostle" comes from the Septuagint, the Greek translation of the Old Testament that Paul used, where the word is used to describe God's prophetic messengers. Apostles are sent with a message from God. So Paul says that he has been appointed by God himself to advance God's plans by announcing the message of Jesus Christ to the world. The Corinthians may still be making their mind up about Paul, but his confidence is firmly in the fact that he has been commissioned by God himself, and that both he, and his sidekick, Timothy, come with God's own authority to speak to what is God's church.

> Leaders are ultimately appointed by Christ and are accountable to Christ.

This is actually the first distinctive of all Christian leadership. It is God who selects, appoints and sends leaders. Leadership is not something we grab or plot to achieve. It is not something we have by right. Character, convictions and competencies are all really important, but even when we have all these things, it doesn't *entitle* us to lead. In the church of Jesus Christ, leaders are ultimately appointed by Jesus Christ and are accountable to Jesus Christ. When any local church appoints leaders, in effect, all they are doing is recognising what God has already done in equipping and shaping leaders for his church. And that's what makes being a leader in the church of Jesus Christ so scary!

Being one of Christ's appointed assistant leaders, if I can put it like that, is a serious thing. That's why leaders in the New Testament are held to such a high standard. Paul writes to Timothy:

"The saying is trustworthy: If anyone aspires to the office of overseer, he desires a noble task. Therefore an **overseer** must be above reproach, the husband of one wife, sober-minded, self-controlled, respectable, hospitable, able to teach."

(1 Timothy 3:1-2)

That's why we need to push those who aspire to be leaders in the church so hard. That's why the work of equipping leaders is a serious business—because in the church, leaders are both appointed by God and held accountable by God, because they are given the job of looking after the church of God. God both rules and provides for his church—which is why Paul writes to "the church of God that is at Corinth" (2 Corinthians **1:1**). We are part of his church rather than him sponsoring ours!

A very irate lady once yelled at me, "You are destroying my church!" I gently pointed out, in a way which was theologically accurate but probably a little bit incendiary, that the church didn't actually belong to her but was the church of the Lord Jesus Christ, and neither she nor I had the right to tell God how to run it; which is basically what Paul says here—the church is the church of God.

Whether we are talking about the group of house churches scattered across Corinth, or add in the rest of the "holy ones", those Jewish and Gentile believers scattered across the rest of southern Greece who were all part of God's **new-covenant** people, or whether we include the local gathering that you are part of, it is the church of God. Our God established it, and he will care for it. As Jesus said, "I will build my church and the gates of hell will not overcome it" (Matthew 16:18). God both *provides for* and *rules* his church—a fact which is underlined by the most overlooked phrase in all of Paul's writing: "Grace to you and peace from God our Father and the Lord Jesus Christ" (2 Corinthians **1:2**).

Grace and peace

In every letter that he writes to a church, Paul opens with this deceptively rich phrase. The word "peace" is instantly understandable to

Jews, with the announcement of *shalom* from God—the promise of the flourishing wellbeing that comes from being in right relationship with the living God. And to both Jews and Gentiles, "grace" declares the undeserved favour of God towards sinners. Paul's formula encapsulates all that God the Father holds out to us in the Lord Jesus Christ through the gospel—*grace and peace*, both of which were in short supply in the turmoil of Corinth.

It would be really easy to skip over this, but we shouldn't because this is a key part of Paul's thinking about the church. Because the church belongs to God and is provided for by God, we have every right to expect the church of the Lord Jesus to be marked by grace and peace. The fact that God has chosen us and rescued us has changed, is changing and will change us. The knowledge of his love for us and the experience of his forgiveness should soften us beyond measure, and make our churches the most accepting and forgiving communities on the planet. And the fact that we have been accepted by God, forgiven, credited with Jesus' **righteousness, sealed with the Spirit** and given the guarantee that he will *never* let us go should cause us to heave a collective sigh of relief, and relax. Our lives as God's people, our life as the church, is to be a life of grace and peace, because the God of grace and peace rules and provides for his church.

It is very easy to overestimate our own importance: to imagine that we have more power, and more significance than we actually do. But if you and I are to be useful in God's kingdom, it is important we realise that there are some things that are beyond us. For a start, we can't actually change anyone. We can't bring people to life, or make them more like Jesus—in fact, we can't even change their minds. *And on top of that, we can't plant, grow and build churches.* Ultimately, that's God's job. The church starts with him, belongs to him, is protected and nurtured by him.

Of course, we need to be wise—we need to make sure that we have the convictions, character and competencies to serve Christ faithfully in our nation and beyond. Of course, we need to make sure we are using the gifts and the wisdom God has given us. But at the end of the day we need to make sure that it has lodged firmly in our skulls that no church we plant or pastor or revitalise or teach or are part of will ever be "mine". We are never more than caretakers of the church that our God has brought to life and cares for more than we will ever imagine.

So I hope you've got this foundation that undergirds all authentic ministry: God rules the church—and he provides for the church in every way, holding out grace and peace in the Lord Jesus. As Paul continues this ongoing battle for the hearts and minds of the people of God in Corinth, he starts with the fact that the church belongs to God. In the rest of our passage, Paul outlines two more key ways in which God holds out his grace and peace to us, his people—ways in which God provides for us, for his church, through the gospel.

The Father of mercies

In **verse 3**, the thought of God showing us grace and peace moves Paul to "benediction"; literally it makes him "speak well" of God. First, he says, "Blessed… be the Father of mercies". The word "mercies" is commonly used in the Old Testament to describe the tender way in which God showers his people with kindness. He then goes on to introduce the key idea in verses 3-7: our God is also the God who offers "comfort" (v 3) in every conceivable situation.

Now I confess that I have a cultural problem in reading this text. When I hear the word "comfort", I am hindered by the fact that the number one brand of fabric softener in the UK and Ireland is called—you guessed it—*Comfort*. The word instantly conjures up hazy images of fluffy towels gently brushing perfect skin, and Labrador puppies gently frolicking in a sea of softness. Comfort for us is a warm and fuzzy word. But for Paul, and for the rest of the New Testament, the word he uses is a long way from warm fuzziness. "Comfort" in the New Testament includes everything from an arm round the shoulder to a kick in the pants!

David E. Garland, New Testament Professor at Baylor University in the US, explains it like this:

"The comfort that Paul has in mind has nothing to do with a languorous feeling of contentment. It is not some tranquilizing dose of grace that only dulls pain but a stiffening agent that fortifies one in heart, mind and soul. Comfort relates to encouragement, help, **exhortation**. God's comfort strengthens weak knees and sustains sagging spirits so that one faces the troubles of life with unbending resolve and unending assurance."

(*2 Corinthians*, p 60)

This is why, in John's Gospel, Jesus himself used the same word to describe the Holy Spirit as the "Comforter", which enfolds the fact that he is the one who convicts us of sin, strengthens us, emboldens us and transforms us. And why does Paul's choice of word matter so much? It matters because it clarifies the very nature of the gospel-driven life and ministry we are all called to.

Living for Jesus is hard. But the great news is that our God—Father, Son and Spirit—is committed to supplying the resources, encouragement, correction and resolve that we need to keep living for him. And that's only the start, as we'll see in part 2.

Questions for reflection

1. Have you grasped the fact that the church belongs to God? Is that reflected in the way you speak about church? Care about church? Treat your brothers and sisters?

2. If leadership is so important, what should we pray for leaders? How should we invest in future leaders?

3. Grace and peace are the twin marks of the local church, according to Paul. Why should the gospel produce these marks? How does that happen?

PART TWO

God comforts us with all comfort in the midst of suffering

In part 1, Paul introduced us to the robust comfort which our merciful God holds out to us. In **verse 4**, Paul now explains that this comfort (or encouragement) is not designed to stop with us. God encourages us in all our affliction, so that we may be able to encourage those who are in any affliction. He makes it so clear that the only thing we have to offer other people is what he has first given us!

> The Christian life is one of suffering and strengthening, of setbacks and encouragement, of struggle and joy.

Paul assumes that the Christian life is one of suffering and strengthening, of setbacks and encouragement, of struggle and joy. That's what we can expect for ourselves and for other people. This is the rhythm of life this side of the new creation. *And so this will always be the reality of ministry.* We face difficulties. God encourages us. Out of God's encouragement of us, we encourage other people. Repeat. This is authentic ministry. God comforts us in all our affliction, so that we may be able to comfort those who are in any affliction, with the comfort with which we ourselves are comforted by God. If you want to be of any use to God, then welcome to the rest of your life.

There are several really significant implications of this template for Christian life and ministry. First, if we take this seriously, then we will be deeply realistic. If this is what life will be like for us, then we need to be prepared for the fact that it will be painful. As we face ourselves, and other people, and our world, all of which are broken, it will be painful. The good news, of course, is that this place of pain and struggle and brokenness is the very place we will receive the encouragement of God through Christ in the gospel. But our lives will still be sore and hard. We need to be very clear on that.

The second implication of this is that when it comes to comforting others, we need to have received the comfort of God in Christ first. We can only share what we have received ourselves. If I can put it slightly differently—if we are to serve Christ, then the comfort of the gospel has to be real and fresh for us. From day to day and week to week, we have to walk this path of struggle and encouragement so that others who watch us and listen to us will be freshly encouraged in the muck of life. That's why we need to keep reading the Bible, on our own and together. That's why we need to speak the gospel into one another's lives. That's why we need to gather as the church to hear the comforting voice of God speaking to us for our encouragement that we might encourage others. God is at work in you and me for the benefit of other people!

Living with and for Jesus is going to be hard, and we need to make sure that we receive comfort before we try to give it, because this is authentic ministry. Grace always comes before service. Are you ready for a life like this? Are you ready to suffer for the benefit of other people? To face pain so that you can offer comfort to the church? Because this is what serving Jesus is all about.

This is both daunting and energising. Not least because it makes it so clear that suffering in all its shapes and forms—your struggle and mine—has a profound purpose for the people of God. In **verses 5-7**, Paul highlights that the only possible outcome of sharing in Christ's sufferings—which I take to mean the "sufferings which come with being associated with Christ"—is encouragement, that is, the strengthening of his people to the glory of Christ. Here's how it works according to Paul—the more we share abundantly in Christ's sufferings, the more comfort we get! The tougher it gets, the better it is for the church of Christ!

Two scenarios

Paul outlines two scenarios—in the first, he and his friends suffer, and the Corinthians are encouraged (**v 6**). In the second, Paul and his friends are encouraged, and the watching Corinthians are encouraged as they go through the same kind of suffering. It's a win-win situation. If we suffer and are encouraged to keep going, then it spurs us on. If you suffer, then you get encouraged directly. God has set things up so that his church thrives when life's hard—which is a good job because, as Jesus said, in this world you will have suffering (John 16:33). Paul now adds that when we suffer in this world, we will also be strengthened—so nobody needs to panic! In fact, when we see others suffer, we can actually be glad because it is a clear sign that God is at work in us and that he will carry us through: "Our hope for you is unshaken for we know that as you share in our sufferings, you will also share in our comfort" (2 Corinthians **1:7**).

It was hard for the churches in Achaia to hear these words. Every fibre of their Corinthian bodies screamed at them that life was about climbing the ladder of honour, respectability and financial security—this has a very modern ring to it. As Paul now seeks to persuade them to hold on to the gospel, and to recognise that their church belongs to God and is ruled by God, he says they must be shaped by God as the gospel of Christ is worked out among them. Paul emphatically impresses on them that life isn't so much an upward march to recognition and prestige as a downward slide together through opposition into disgrace. But as we slide together, we will find immeasurable strength and unimagined encouragement! This has been Paul's lived experience—he knows this is how it works—and he calls them and us to join him in this experience of authentic Christian life and ministry. This is an impassioned plea to the Corinthians to stick with Paul, and press on with Paul, and suffer with Paul as together they live for the God of the gospel.

This is the life God calls us to—one of encouraging and being encouraged in the midst of suffering. Like the Corinthians, many of us feel the allure of success. Paul tells us to aim higher—how about we focus on staying faithful through suffering? Why? Because these simple statements make it so clear that no experience is wasted in God's flawless economy. Your suffering and mine leads to encouragement for us and for other people. And when we live together like that, we discover that there is nothing more precious than fellowship forged in suffering, as God comforts us with all comfort in the midst of it all.

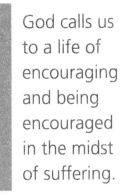

God calls us to a life of encouraging and being encouraged in the midst of suffering.

I was a pastor in Dublin for twelve years, where the senior **Elder** in our church was a man called Garvin Evans. Garvin was as good a friend and supporter as anyone could ever ask for. We went through some pretty rough times together. And in the midst of those times, he would often phone and say "Hello Gary, this is your "friend in battle", which, as he would regularly remind me, is what the name Garvin means in Welsh. Garvin has gone to be with the Lord now, but I still thank God for him and his friendship for those were tough times, but I can also tell you that those were also some of the sweetest times I have known, as our God comforted us with all comfort though suffering. This is the way in which our God works. But that's not all.

God will deliver us (in the end)

One of the key challenges that Paul—and the progress of the gospel—faced in Corinth was the almost overwhelming cultural pressure to impress: to look good, to sound good and to enjoy the good life here and now. The apostle's ongoing battle was to persuade the church to listen to him, and stick with him, as he promised comfort in suffering now, and the future glory that will come through the death and resurrection of Jesus. It seems that every visit and every letter was designed to help the Corinthians grasp this and hold on to the reality that Jesus' death and resurrection has changed everything. It not only frees us up to be honest and realistic about the present but completely revolutionises our future. It seems that, finally, Paul is winning the battle for their hearts and minds—but if they are going to hang in with him, then Paul knows they need to be utterly convinced not only that there is purpose in suffering now, but that there is hope beyond suffering. And that's where Paul goes in **verses 8-11**.

In his letters, Paul tends to veer away from talking about himself, but not here. In verses 8-11 he does exactly what he has just described in verses 4-7. He shares what God has taught him for the encouragement of others. And why does he do it here? He makes a point of telling the Corinthians that he was falling apart, facing death, because he knows that, given any opportunity they will slip into thinking about ministry in terms of success and giftedness and honour and impressiveness—so he reminds them over and over again that real gospel ministry is born of encouragement in suffering, an encouragement which ultimately flows from the fact that God will rescue us from this body of death, to live with him for ever.

Look at what he says in **verses 8-9**. Paul's language here is pretty extreme. He speaks of his "affliction", of being "utterly burdened beyond our strength" and of despairing of life so that he felt that he had received a death sentence. His point is that every cry for help was knocked back, and as a result, despair would have been the easiest thing to feel. Paul is not just saying he was having a rough week. He was right on the edge. Ambrosiaster, in his 4th-century commentary on this letter, writes that "Paul means that there was such a violent upsurge of evil against preachers of the faith that death was staring them in the face". That pretty much nails it.

That's how Paul continues in the second half of **verse 10**—*God has delivered me … he will deliver us again … he will continue to deliver us!* Our regular experience of God working in and through our suffering, rescuing us time after time, until we get to the point when he calls us home, is the testimony that our future is utterly secure in

Christ. It is also the way in which God reminds us over and over again that our hope rests in him alone, and that one day, rather than helping us to cope through our suffering or rescuing us from our suffering, he will bring us out of suffering to be with him for ever. The Corinthians needed to finally concede the fact that going through suffering, rather than something to be avoided at all costs, teaches us to put our trust in God. In fact, they needed to learn that there is no other way of learning to entrust ourselves and our futures to God.

Because of the cultural air that they breathe, the Christians in Corinth are prone to thinking that with gifted people and good preaching they can pull it off. They aren't entirely sure that Paul, with all his downbeat talk about suffering, and his plain speaking and lack of **rhetorical** polish is the kind of man they need as a leader. So what does Paul do? Paul says, *Yes—you're right—I've got nothing. You want an impressive resumé? All I can show you are my bruises. All I can do is list the occasions I've been run out of town. All I can boast about is the fact that God has rescued me from death. But it isn't about me—or you for that matter. It's about our God, who shows us our weakness, encourages us through weakness, and will rescue us through the gospel of the Lord Jesus. So have you got that? Are you with me?*

Paul tells them about his own near-death experience to remind them that only the message of the cross can give them hope in the face of death. There is nothing like panic and helplessness to strengthen our trust in God our rescuer. There is nothing like suffering and danger to remind us that God alone is our hope.

John Calvin expresses this beautifully:

"First, the fleshly confidence by which we are puffed up is so obstinate that the only way it can be destroyed is by our falling into extremes of despair. For the flesh is proud and does not yield willingly so that its pretensions cease only when it is forcibly constrained. We are not brought to real submission until we have been laid low by the crushing hand of God. Second, we should note that the remnants of this disease of pride linger even in the saints, so that they too often need to be reduced to extremities in order to be stripped of all their self-confidence and learn humility. The roots of this evil are so deep in the human heart that even the most perfect among us are never entirely free of it, till God confronts them with death. We may gather how much our self-confidence displeases God when we see how, in order to cure it, we have to be condemned to death."

(*The Second Epistle of Paul to the Corinthians*, p 12-13)

Unusually at this point, Paul asks the Corinthians to pray for him (v 11), so that when their prayers are answered, "many will give thanks on our behalf for the blessing granted us through the prayers of many". It's pretty clear that Paul is working so hard to draw them in, to deepen their partnership, so now he throws in the need to pray for one another. In a way, it's a further application of verses 4-5. We pray for each other as we suffer for the gospel; and as we see God doing what he has promised and what we have asked him to do, strengthening us to live the gospel, then we in turn are encouraged—until that day when God brings us home to be together. Verses 8-11 are the pointy end of Paul's appeal to the Corinthians to stick with him for the gospel for the long haul. He is urging them to throw their lot in with him as partners in the gospel.

> We are all responsible for our own actions, of course, but we desperately need each other.

This is what God calls us to together. We are all responsible for our own actions, of course, but we desperately need each other—to pray for one another, to encourage one another, to learn from one another, to love one another and to spur one another on. For a day is coming when God will deliver us together to enjoy God together for ever. That's why community matters so much. That's why gospel partnership between local churches, whatever the denomination, matters. That's why gospel partnership across our cities,and states and nations matters so much: because we are the church of God, and we are in this together, and our God will bring us home together.

This is the ministry that God invites us to share in. How could we possibly settle for anything else?

Questions for reflection

1. Reflect on the fact that God is already committed to giving us whatever "comfort" we need to live for him together this week. What difference does this make? Where should we expect to find this "comfort"? If we aren't being "comforted by God", what is the knock-on effect in the life of the church?

2. How can our suffering encourage other people?

3. Why does it make a difference that God will deliver us in the end?

2. A MATTER OF TRUST

Why should I trust you? And come to think of it—why should you trust me? These questions are at the heart of this passage, which runs from 2 Corinthians 1:12 to 2:12. And it's all because Paul said one thing, and did another.

The problem was that Paul had said he was coming to Corinth, and then he didn't show up. We'll see more of the details in a moment. But the end result of Paul's action is very serious. Even as the Corinthians were whining—*But you promised*—it's clear that Paul's change in travel plans had seriously damaged their long and messy relationship with the apostle. In fact, their relationship was at breaking point. They were in real danger of walking away from Paul and, even worse, walking away from the gospel. So Paul writes to them once more, pleading with them to do one thing: he says, *TRUST ME!*

There's a sense in which once you've got that, you've got this passage. And we could almost stop there. Almost. If it weren't for the fact that Paul goes on to explain why they should trust him in a way that takes us right to the heart of what it means to be a Christ-like leader. In fact, it takes us right to the heart of what it means to be a Christian. So, at the risk of spoiling the surprise, here's his answer to the question "Why should you trust me?" Paul replies, *Because I'm imitating Christ.* He says, *Trust me because I trust Christ. The basis for trust between you and me—the basis for trust in the church of Jesus Christ is Christ-likeness.*

Now I know that we are all deeply sinful, and that even though we have been forgiven and made holy, and are being transformed by Christ, we never quite escape the down-drag of our sin. You will hear plenty more about that in this letter. But we must never let the importance of a robust grasp on the **doctrine** of sin obliterate the fact that we are also called to be holy—to live Christ-like lives. And more than that, we cannot ignore the fact that all of us are equipped to, and expected to, copy and resemble the Lord Jesus Christ himself.

This isn't a new idea for the Corinthians—back in 1 Corinthians 4:16 Paul had written, "I urge you, then, be imitators of me". He'd done it again in 11:1: "Be imitators of me, as I am of Christ". This is the bedrock of Paul's appeal to the Corinthians in this letter too: *Stick with me and the gospel, come with me, copy me as I copy Christ.*

I don't know about you, but I have always felt just a little bit uncomfortable with this. In most cultures it is considered socially unacceptable to bignote or brag about yourself. *Look at me—this is how to follow Jesus!* And yet, there is a sense in which, whether we like it or not, this is the pattern of gospel-shaped ministry. We are called to live like Jesus, lead like Jesus, to imitate Jesus—even if our imitation is often pretty pathetic. And Paul seems to think that this responsibility weighs even more heavily on leaders.

So our trajectory for this chapter is set—Paul's argument is built on the conviction that ministry and Christ-likeness are inseparable, and that if you look at his life, that will be blatantly obvious. *Feeling guilty yet?* Crawling **metaphorically** under your seat because you aren't quite convinced that if your life was held up to public scrutiny, Christ-likeness is the first word that would jump into everyone's mind? But fear not. The great beauty of this passage is that it doesn't simply call us to an impossibly high standard but also throws us back on Christ himself, in whom God has given us everything we need for life and godliness.

Paul's response to the concern, and perhaps even accusations, of the Corinthians—his defence and his plea for them to trust him—comes in four broad movements, as he highlights four marks of his life, which, it turns out, are all deeply Christ-like.

Four Marks of Christ-likeness
Mark 1: Transparent sincerity

In his novel *The Scarlet Letter*, Nathaniel Hawthorne wrote, "A pure hand needs no glove to cover it". And that's Paul's basic contention in this section. He says, *When it comes to me, what you see is what you get.*

Now there are a pile of minor problems in these verses, but they are all relatively easily resolved. The first is the idea of boasting. For us, boasting has an entirely negative connotation. There is no such thing as good boasting. But for Paul, eight times out of ten, boasting is a marvellous thing. How can this be? Because Paul is boasting about what God has done in Christ, and then in us. That's crucial to understanding what Paul is doing here. Everything he says here is based on the premise that he is what he is by the grace of God, as he spells out at the end of **verse 12**.

> This chapter doesn't simply call us to an impossibly high standard but also throws us back on Christ himself.

To understand Paul's boasting—and, in fact, to understand his transparent sincerity—we need to understand how Paul's identity has been utterly reshaped by his encounter with Christ in the gospel. He has been rebooted by the grace of God. His view of himself and the world, his decision-making processes, the way in which he relates to others have all been completely realigned, reoriented by the unconditional love and extravagant, undeserved kindness that God has held out to him in the Lord Jesus. This has changed the whole **key signature** of his life. Of course he is not yet perfect, but he is different.

The fact that Christ completely relocates our identity has seldom been captured with such balance and power as in these oft-quoted words of John Newton, of "Amazing Grace" fame: Newton wrote:

"I am not what I ought to be. Ah! How imperfect and deficient! I am not what I wish to be. I abhor what is evil, and I would cleave to what is good. I am not what I hope to be. Soon, soon, I shall put off mortality, and with mortality all sin and imperfection. Yet, though I am not what I ought to be, nor what I wish to be, nor what I hope to be, I can truly say, I am not what I once was—a slave to sin and Satan. And I can heartily join with the apostle, and acknowledge, 'By the grace of God, I am what I am'."

(Josiah Bull, *The Life of John Newton*, p 289)

It is because of this transforming grace that Paul can boast in line with "the testimony of [his] conscience". As Christopher Ash points out in his really important book on the conscience, *Pure Joy*, the conscience is the highly sensitive, slightly unreliable instrument that convicts us of the gap between what the Bible says and how we are living.

"Conscience detects where our lives don't match with what we say we believe. And even though our conscience is easily desensitised, and hardened, when we become Christians, the Spirit instantly begins to repair our damaged conscience, with the result that it is actually possible for us to have clear conscience in specific situations and on specific issues. And that's what Paul is saying. If we examine ourselves honestly before God in the light of his word, it is possible to speak with quiet confidence and real humility about our actions, which is what Paul does—that we behaved in the world with simplicity and godly sincerity, not by earthly wisdom but by the grace of God, and supremely so toward you."

(*Pure Joy: Rediscover your Conscience*)

The word "behaved" in verse 12 is also an unusual one, which Paul has chosen because it conveys the idea of a pattern of behaviour, rather than individual actions. He's not implying that he has reached a state of sinless perfection, or that every individual action he takes is utterly free from any taint of selfishness or mixed motives. This is a "big picture" statement, saying that his actions have been character-ised by transparent sincerity—or to use his own words—"simplicity and godly sincerity". There were plenty of people in Corinth passing through on the ancient "stand-up philosophy" circuit who may have been making a living from what he calls "earthly wisdom". They were very happy to talk themselves up, play to the crowd and line their own pockets. But not Paul—because he has been recalibrated by the grace of God. And that means that with Paul, what you see is what you get. He is transparently, wholeheartedly sincere. And that really is the way it should be.

He underlines that in **verses 13-14**. He wasn't showing off—he wrote and spoke to help the Corinthians get the truth about Jesus, so that "on the day of our Lord Jesus you will boast of us as we will boast of you". Paul keeps banging on about the same thing: *Because of Christ we are in this together. We suffer together for him. We encourage each other together in him. We will be brought home together by him.* Now Paul knows they haven't quite got this yet—but he longs for them to get it, and to get to the place where they can boast about what our Lord Jesus has done in the lives of others to his glory.

Of course, all this can only happen if God works in us through the Spirit of Christ. It is Jesus Christ who produces in us this straightforwardness, this transparent sincerity. An integrity and wholeheartedness which isn't always trying to impress, or talk ourselves up, or manipulate, or dominate, or flatter, or mislead. But an authenticity which lives and breathes that "By the grace of God, I am what I am".

So would people in your family or your church family or your work colleagues or neighbours say that you are straightforwardly open, wholehearted and sincere? It's a good question to ask. And of course, the problem with sincerity is that, by its very nature, it's almost impossible to fake. For some reason, most of us have an innate ability to smell pretence and fakery. We know the real deal when we see it. And what is the real deal? Authentic transparent sincerity that can only be produced by the grace of God in Christ.

Mark 2: Dependable flexibility

Because Paul is convinced that God has called us to suffer together, to encourage one another, and to boast in what God is doing in each other, he is utterly committed to pursuing his relationship with the Corinthians. That's why he keeps writing. That's why he keeps visiting them—and planning more visits (**v 15-16**).

It's not entirely clear whether Paul had intended a double visit in order to give them two opportunities to give to his appeal for funds to support the struggling church back in Jerusalem, or whether he just meant they would get to see each other twice. But either way, it's striking how Paul's motivation is that his travel plans would lead to the encouragement of God's people wherever they were. He says a similar thing in Romans 1:9-12, where he wants to visit Rome is so that he...

"... may impart to you some spiritual gift [literally: *grace*] to strengthen you—that is, that we may be mutually encouraged by each other's faith, both yours and mine."

> Gospel people are dependable because God is completely dependable.

Grace produced a gospel-shaped dependability in Paul. His grip on the message of the gospel itself was firm, and you could count on him to spend himself for the good of the church. The problem was that when he hadn't shown up, the Corinthians had accused him of being flaky, unreliable and unstable. But Paul goes on to explain that gospel people need to be dependable, of course, but also flexible.

He explains in 2 Corinthians 1:**17-19** that his change of plan wasn't because he doesn't keep his commitments but because circumstances changed. Paul's basic point is that gospel people (including him) are dependable because God is completely dependable. That's why Paul makes the towering statement in **verse 20**: "For all the promises of God find their Yes in him [Christ]". Because God has shown himself to be utterly dependable in Christ, Paul and his companions can be depended upon to put the gospel of Christ first, which will mean, at times, being flexible and reordering their priorities to serve the gospel good.

Now let me say quickly that this is not an excuse for being disorganised or unreliable. Calvin says:

"There are two main reasons why men's plans are not successfully accomplished or their promises faithfully kept. The first is that they change their minds almost hourly, and the second that they are too hasty in the commitments they undertake. It is a sign of instability to make plans or promises you immediately regret."

(*The Second Epistle of Paul to the Corinthians*, p 19)

And Paul would agree—this is exactly the kind of thing he is distancing himself from. He is trustworthy because he belongs to a trustworthy God! This is why he would never say "Absolutely" in one breath and "No way" in the next (**v 18**). His priorities are always gospel priorities—when it comes to the advance of the gospel, it was never *Yes and No*, but in Christ it is always *Yes*. Jesus was resolutely dependable in saying "Not my will but yours", and Paul is following in his steps. Jesus Christ was faithful to and through death—which is why the fulfilment of all God's promises is found in him. He was utterly dependable and did exactly what God asked of him. All God's covenant promises have reached their crescendo with Jesus Christ as their resolute answer.

So what, then, are we to do? How are we to respond? **Verse 20**— we are to answer his faithfulness with our own, uttering "our Amen to God for his glory". Because we can rely on God, this leads us into a gospel reliability (**verses 21-22**). When the gospel is our absolute priority, we will be predictably, reliably faithful to the gospel, even if it means that our plans may change when the progress of the gospel demands it. And how can we pull that off? Once again, it's because God hasn't simply *told us* to be like Christ; he has intervened in our lives powerfully and dramatically *to enable us* to be like Christ. He strengthens us in real time, having anointed us and sealed us with the Spirit—God guaranteeing that he will complete his work in us. This is what God in his grace has already done for us and put within our reach in Christ.

So are you dependably flexible? Can you be counted on to put the gospel first, and to arrange your life around whatever priorities the gospel brings to you in your situation? George Guthrie, in his brilliant commentary on 2 Corinthians, sums it up like this:

"Paul's mission, his decisions, his pattern of life, and therefore his words are not perfect, but they so rest on the bedrock of the character of God, and are so in sync with God's gospel, that Paul can speak of the integrity of his words and commitments with the utmost confidence."

(*2 Corinthians*, p 110)

And this is the shape of the grace which God makes available to us.

Questions for reflection

1. Why should gospel-driven people be deeply trustworthy?

2. The call to be like Christ is impossibly daunting—so how come it isn't depressing but exciting for Paul?

3. How can people like us (who have much to hide) live in a way which is both transparent and sincere?

PART TWO

In 1:23-2:13, we get to the nub of Paul's explanation of why he *doesn't* come back to Corinth. It's because he loves them. Because he loves them deeply, he IS prepared to stay away because he knows that showing up again right after the "painful visit" would only make things worse.

The apostle walks them through this, starting at **1:23**:

"But I call God to witness against me [literally: *against my life*]—it was to spare you that I refrained from coming again to Corinth."

Paul knew that if he showed up again, he was going to have to confront and correct them again, at a time when they were still raw from his last visit. And that wasn't because he was a nasty person, or too blunt or demanding—on the contrary, according to **verse 24**, his preoccupation is their joy, and his goal is that they stand firm in their faith. Because Paul loves people, once they have understood the gospel and are "standing firm in [their] faith", his overwhelming concern is that they taste the real and solid joy of the gospel. Which takes us to the third mark of Christ-likeness which shapes this entire section.

Mark 3: Robust love

One of the chief aims and marks of the gospel-shaped life is that we love people enough to spend ourselves to engender joy in those we serve. Of course, God alone can produce real joy, but how does he do that? He does it by the Spirit through the ministry of the gospel, to which he calls *us*! John Piper writes:

"This is why gladness and gravity should be woven together in the life and preaching of a pastor ... love for people does not take precious realities lightly (hence the call for gravity) and love for people does not load people with the burden of obedience without providing the strength of joy to help them carry it (hence the call for gladness)."

(*The Supremacy of God in Preaching*, p 52)

This is echoing precisely what Paul says here. In all his ministry, he is urging people to embrace both the seriousness and the satisfaction of the gospel, and his goal is to see people delight in God. This is what robust love looks like. So do you love the people in your church? The people you sit alongside, the people you serve, the people who teach you, the people you teach? If you do, then you will be preoccupied with them and weighed down by the responsibility of leading, pushing and prodding them into joy in Christ. You'll be ready to do anything to help them know that joy, and you will be willing to refrain from doing anything which would deflect them from the gospel faithfulness which leads to this joy. For this is what Christ-like love looks like. It is love which understands that my joy and yours are organically connected.

That jumps out of what Paul says in 2:1-4. He knew that if he had come and caused more pain, they would have all been miserable (**v 1**). He feels the acute discomfort of being robbed of the joy of seeing them flourish, and of not being able to share his own joy in Christ with them (**verses 2-3**). This was a deeply painful situation for him. That's the spirit in which he wrote, sending the letter "out of much affliction and anguish of heart and with many tears, not to cause you pain but to let you know the abundant love that I have for you" (**v 4**). Paul had thought through his change of itinerary carefully and lovingly, because he was working for their greatest and lasting joy, which was also what brought him real joy in Christ—so instead of coming in person, he wrote a gut-wrenching, heart-breaking, tear-stained, love-saturated letter.

> Paul is urging people to embrace both the seriousness and the satisfaction of the gospel.

I can't read these words without being chastened and confronted by the weakness of my own care for people. Calvin's commentary on these verses penetrate my heart:

"There are many noisy scolders who display an amazing fervour in denouncing and raging against other people's faults and yet are untouched at heart so that they seem to take pleasure in exercising their throat and lungs. But it belongs to a godly pastor to weep within himself before he makes others weep, to suffer in his own secret heart before he gives any open sign of his wrath, and to keep to himself more grief than he causes to others."

(The Second Epistle of Paul to the Corinthians, p 28)

This is Christ-like ministry.

My wife, Fiona, and I have three precious daughters. I don't think they would mind us saying that they are the source of the greatest joy and the greatest concern in our lives. That's the territory where love operates, and so this is what it's like to live together for the gospel. To follow Jesus is to walk in the steps of the One who wept over Jerusalem. Who wept at the grave of his friend Lazarus. Who sweat drops of blood at the prospect of dying in our place. Who went to his death on a cross for us. This is the strong love that God has shown us, and the strong love that God has called us to.

Surprisingly, Paul gives further evidence of the warmth of his love for the church in Corinth and his preoccupation with their joy in verses 5-11, as he turns to a very specific Corinthian issue. Previously, Paul had encouraged them to deal firmly with someone who had sinned spectacularly and publicly (probably the events alluded to in 1 Corinthians 5:1-5). Paul has heard, to his encouragement, that they did this. But now, tough old Paul, the one who was so insistent on **church discipline**, tells them that enough is enough: not because of any personal agenda, but because of the need for the whole church, hurt by this sin (2 Corinthians **2:5**), to experience and embrace the healing that flows from **repentance**. Now that discipline has been exercised (**v 6**), and the person brought to repentance, Paul tells the church in **verse 7** to turn to forgive and comfort him, or he may be overwhelmed by excessive sorrow (literally: "swallowed up by sin"). This really is the softer side of Paul—his love is robust, but it is also tender, as he urges them to "reaffirm your love for him" (**v 8**). Nothing is brushed under the carpet, but nor is this discipline vindictive—or even permanent. Church discipline for Paul has the goal of repentance and restoration, and that is the possibility before the church.

In fact, Paul presses on to urge the Corinthians to show that they really have grasped the gospel and are living in the light of the gospel: to demonstrate it in grace and forgiveness. His earlier letter had functioned as a test of their wholeheartedness (**v 9**). *Are you really on board with a gospel agenda?* This was Paul's concern. He has no vendetta against the individual concerned. He is eager to move on in forgiveness (**v 10**). He knows that taking the easy way out and ignoring church discipline on the one hand (which is probably a more common problem), and becoming harsh and condemning on the other plays right into Satan's hands, as he spells out in **verse 11**, in undermining the witness of the church and the ministry of the gospel.

The absence of church discipline in many of our churches, then, may actually be an indictment of our lack of love for one another, flowing from a shallow grasp of the love which God has shown us in Christ. The lack of robust love expressed as godly, graceful discipline is one of the great challenges that we face in this generation. This lack lies at the root of all kinds of issues, from covering up abuse to losing any concept of church belonging and membership. Think how striking it would be in our world if we dealt well with both sin and repentance, showing the kind of forgiveness and restoration that John Chrysostom described in the 4th century:

> "Reveal your friendship as certain, unshakable, fervent, ardent and fiery; present your love with the same strength as the previous hatred."   (*On Repentance and Almsgiving*, 1.3.22)

This is robust love. Godly love. Love which can be trusted.

Mark 4: Real care

If you haven't picked up yet that Paul really does care about people, look at what he says in **2:12-13**. Paul was in Troas—the crossroads where he had to make up his mind whether to go to Corinth or not, and where two things happened. First, he had the opportunity to take the gospel to Macedonia (to Philippi and the other places recounted in Acts 15 – 18)—that's what he means by the door which opened for him. And secondly, there was no sign of Titus, who had arranged to meet him in Troas, and Paul was desperately worried.

It's fairly clear that Paul saw that he could respond to both of these situations by going to Macedonia, to preach and to look for Titus. His double motivation was preaching the gospel and care for his friend and partner in the gospel, Titus—whom he did find there. Why does Paul include this detail? To make clear that for him he isn't simply focused on the gospel message; but, because of the gospel, he is a people person as well.

> Because of the gospel, Paul is a people person.

One of the astonishing things about the Lord Jesus is his consistent, extravagant care for people—the Gospels are packed with people who encounter Jesus and find that he knows them, cares for them and speaks right into their lives. And the apostle Paul is no different. His letters are full of names, generally of people with whom he has formed strong bonds and is genuinely concerned for. For him Christ-like ministry means really caring for the people he works with—in this case, Titus—and those whom he serves.

Unfortunately, many of us don't excel at this kind of loving brotherly and sisterly commitment to partners in the gospel. We tend not to function as brothers-in-arms who will happily drop everything to run to a friend's aid, especially when the cause of the gospel is involved. And yet this very real care, this brotherly affection, this deep partnership was a mark both of Jesus' ministry and of Paul's. Which raises an important question: *what kind of brother or sister are you going to be? What kind of colleague or leader are you going to be in the years ahead?*

You could, of course, just put your head down and devote yourself to your own life and ministry, in your own place, doing it your way. Or you could serve with your head up and your heart open. Taking the time to drop in to see how the others in your Bible-study group are doing. Flicking an email or sending a message to make sure that they know that they are not alone, because you care. Of course, this will make life tougher—anxiety and concern go with this kind of gospel partnership. It demands real-time effort and practical steps. But it's worth it.

Can you imagine how much it must have meant to Titus that Paul was willing to change his travel plans to make sure that he was ok? Those are the kind of friends we need to keep us going. Friends who don't assume that everything is ok. Friends who take time to work out the kind of encouragement we need. Friends who notice when we're not quite firing on all cylinders. Don't we all need friends like that? Don't you want to be a friend like that? This is the real care that flows from a deep commitment to loving one another as partners in gospel ministry.

Living the real deal

Remember, Paul writes this because he desperately wants the Corinthians to stop messing about and start trusting him because they get the fact that his ministry is the real deal, and he is the real deal, because the gospel he preaches is the real deal.

It is God, through the gospel, who produces people and ministry marked by transparent simplicity, dependable flexibility, robust love and real care. So as those who want to serve the church of Christ in the years ahead, our greatest need is to run to him, follow him, look to him, and drink in his teaching and presence, confident that he will supply our every need. To follow Paul as he follows Christ. But in doing so, we are not merely following a human leader. In the words of 2 Corinthians **1:21**, we are following "God who establishes us with you in Christ, and has anointed us, and who has also put his seal on us and given us his Spirit in our hearts as a guarantee".

Questions for reflection

1. What produces real love for our brothers and sisters? What might this look like in your context this week?

2. Is "robust" a helpful word to pair with "love" when speaking of relationships in church? Why?

3. What's the connection between practical care and the gospel?

3. COME AND JOIN THE PARADE

Do you ever wake up in the morning and say to yourself "I really don't think I can do this"? You may feel overwhelmed by the sheer volume of what you have to get through. You may be plagued with self-doubt. Or it may be even worse than that—you may be grappling with a deep sense of self-loathing. You know that you are a hypocrite and a fraud. And you have a gnawing suspicion that it's only a matter of time before everyone else catches on, and you are exposed. Whatever the particular flavour of your insecurities, I suspect that most believers, if not all of us, question from time to time whether we have what it takes for life as an authentic, selfless follower of the Lord Jesus Christ. And if that's you, then let me tell you that we're in good company.

As we have seen in the previous chapters, Paul has just poured out his heart to the Corinthians, urging them to trust him and to trust his gospel. He has just played his highest card: he has insisted that he is sincere, dependable, loving and motivated by the gospel—calling them to imitate him as he imitates Christ. He knows this is a risky strategy. It would be so easy to get the idea that Paul is setting himself up as something special (see 1:12-14). Which is why in 2:14 – 3:18, Paul goes to enormous lengths to make it very clear that the only reason he is up to the task of serving Christ is because God himself stands behind him.

If we want to set ourselves up to keep pressing on and serving Jesus wholeheartedly for the long haul, then this passage is the ideal place to start. In this section, through Paul, God gives us three reasons why we do not need to be ashamed, embarrassed or crippled by self-doubt, fear or even shame, but can get on with serving Christ by speaking the gospel, come what may.

Reason 1: Because God speaks through us when we speak the gospel

The key question for Paul is right at the heart of this paragraph in **verse 16**: "who is sufficient for these things?" The surprising thing is that Paul's answer isn't "nobody", but "we are"! And how can he say that? Because of the power of the gospel. Our sufficiency, our adequacy, our qualification for the task has nothing to do with us, thank God, but it flows from the fact that God speaks through his words as he speaks the gospel message.

> God speaks through his words as he speaks the gospel message.

Unlike the travelling philosophers, who could make a healthy income by charging for their "services" when they came to town, Paul insists that he (along with his companions, and by extension, all servants of Christ) speak as "men of sincerity, as commissioned by God" (**v 17**). The reason for this distinctive approach is spelled out at the end of verse 17: "in the sight of God we speak in Christ". Speaking before God, in Christ—speaking in a way which is marked by the sincerity that comes from knowing we are accountable to God, and by the depth of insight and knowledge that comes to us through our union with Christ—is what makes inadequate people like us adequate for this task: an insight which is filled out by Paul's description of a parade in **verses 14-16**.

Paul paints a picture of the familiar splendour of a Roman *pompa triumphalis*, the victory parade granted to particularly successful generals. Over 300 of these events are recorded in Graeco-Roman literature. Most commentators and translations are agreed that this is what this passage is referring to. What isn't so clear is where we fit into this scene.

There were seven key components in most of these processions.

- First in the *pompa triumphalis* came a group carrying pictures of the great battle and boards carrying the names of conquered cities and nations, as well as some of the plundered riches of those defeated.

- Then came some white bulls to be sacrificed to Jupiter.

- Third came the conquered peoples. In many cases, the key leaders of these people were taken to the Temple of Jupiter and executed at the end of this "happy" celebration.

- Fourth in line were a group of incense-bearers producing clouds of smoke.

- Then the successful general (the *triumphator*) appeared at the heart of the parade in fifth position.

- In the wake of the victorious general came two more groups—in sixth position came those Romans, presumably now intensely grateful, who had been rescued from the barbarians in this campaign.

- And then, the general's own troops brought up the rear in seventh position.

Normally, attempts to make sense of this scene seek to identify us with one of those seven groups—most often, as reflected in the NIV for example, with the prisoners: "God who always leads us as captives in Christ's triumphal procession". There is however a slight problem with that—the captives in this procession were generally about to be executed by the one whom the parade was honouring, which would be a very unusual (not to say depressing) picture of Christian discipleship! So how can we make sense of this? The key actually lies in the group of people in the parade who are often overlooked. It's the incense-bearers, who, for Paul, are the most important group of all.

Appian of Alexandria wrote this at the turn of the first century, describing just such a procession:

> "Next came a large number of incense-bearers, and just after the fragrances, the general himself on a chariot inscribed with various designs, wreathed in gold and precious stones…"

Similarly Dionysius of Halicarnassus wrote:

> "After them [came] the people taking care of the incense censers in which aromatic herbs and frankincense were burned to produce fragrant smoke along the whole route."

> (Quoted, along with many other ancient parallels, in
> George Guthrie, *2 Corinthians*, p 166)

Now look again at what Paul actually writes, as he give thanks to God, "who in Christ always leads us in triumphal procession" (**v 14**). Christ is identified *with* God the Father as the *triumphator*—the victorious general. Then we are clearly identified as the incense-bearers, as "through us *[he]* spreads the fragrance of the knowledge of him everywhere". It is our role to spread the knowledge of God in Christ, which, for Paul, always happens through the proclamation of the gospel.

Paul presses the image to say that not only are we the incense-carriers, we are actually the smell itself, which has its source in Christ and rises up to honour God himself. As incense-bearers in the parade, spreading the pungent smell of the gospel, we are actually "the aroma of Christ to God" (**v 15**). This gospel proclamation takes place *among those who are being saved and among those who are perishing,* which is clearly a reference to the two key groups in the *pompa triumphalis*. According to **verse 16**, this gospel is breathed in both by those who have opposed the general and have been defeated (and are, perhaps, even about to be executed)—to these people our message and our very presence is the stench of death—and by those who have been rescued by the general and are skipping along, delighting in their newly restored freedom and even life.

Notice where Paul goes with this. This is very definitely not Paul's version of the desperately misleading bumper-sticker slogan wrongly attributed to Francis of Assisi—"Preach the gospel—when necessary use words". Paul is not saying, *Just allow the aroma of your life to permeate society*. There is no warrant here or anywhere else in the New Testament for saying all that we need to do is smell for Jesus! In fact, Paul is saying the reverse: we are up to the task of gospel preaching, if we will simply speak the truth as men of sincerity: "as commissioned by God, in the sight of God we speak in Christ". According to Lucian, a 2nd-century Syrian writer, "The philosophers sell their teaching like tavern keepers, and most of them mix their wine with water and misrepresent it", (*Hermotimus, 59.*179), but not Paul and not us. Instead we spread the fragrance of Christ by speaking the gospel of Christ, knowing that God speaks through us when we speak the gospel.

It is also highly likely that Paul depicts us as the incense bearers because being an incense-bearer didn't require a terribly high degree of expertise. All you really needed to do as an incense-bearer was walk along and let the fragrance waft! Perhaps you needed to blow the smoke occasionally, or fan it in the direction of the crowds, but that's about it. The incense-bearer doesn't have to create the aroma—he or she just shows up and holds up the incense, and the smoke does the rest! And this is the role that God gives to us. Are we up to the task of gospel ministry? If we are prepared to speak in the power of Christ about Christ with sincerity, then yes we are—because it is God who speaks through us when we speak the gospel.

> Who is sufficient for this? We are—because God speaks through the gospel.

Who is sufficient for this? *We are*—because God speaks through the gospel. It would be good to remember that the next time you think that you have nothing to say to your friends who aren't Christians. It would be good to remember that the next time you are fighting a sense of dread in your stomach before you speak in church, and a voice screams in your head, "Who do you think you are? Do you really think anyone is going to pay attention to this?" The great news is that the task of gospel proclamation isn't really about us. Our sufficiency for gospel ministry isn't based on us; it's based on the fragrance of Christ, which God himself spreads through the gospel. We have nothing else. Living a gospel-shaped life as we serve Christ isn't about us. Or our personality. Or our giftedness. Or our knowledge. It is about God speaking in Christ through us.

> Jesus Christ has already won the definitive victory over sin, death and Satan.

This short paragraph is one of the most encouraging, freeing and motivating passages in the entire New Testament. It guards us on the one hand from slipping into thinking that evangelism is too hard for us (or that somehow we aren't qualified for the task which God calls us to), and on the other, it reminds us that ultimately it is God's work to bring people to new life in the power of the Spirit through the gospel of Christ. The Lord Jesus Christ has already won the definitive victory over sin, death and Satan, and it is our role and privilege to spread that powerful news in our world, as God works in salvation and judgment. That's the first reason we can forget about ourselves and get on with serving Christ.

Questions for reflection

1. How does God speak to us? What difference does this make to the way in which we do evangelism?

2. If we are "incense-bearers", what are our responsibilities when it comes to evangelism?

3. Why does Paul go to great lengths to explain that the message of the gospel brings both life and death?

PART TWO

In 2:13-17, Paul explains that we can be confident in our evangelism because God speaks through the gospel. In 3:1-11, Paul adds a second and a third reason not to be ashamed.

Reason 2: Because God changes people through the gospel

You can see from **3:5** that the question which he raised in 2:16 is still on Paul's mind: how do we know we are up to this? The second part of his answer is very clear: we aren't sufficient in ourselves to claim anything as coming from us, but our sufficiency is from God. This adequacy or qualification flows from the fact that God himself has *made us sufficient to be ministers of a new covenant* (**3:6**). His point, as we're about to see, is that God not only speaks but *changes people* through the gospel. And that means that, despite all our inadequacy, we can keep going and get on with the job. Paul fleshes that out by talking first about the way in which God has changed the Corinthians themselves in **verses 1-4**, and then the kind of ministry that God has given all of us through Christ in **verses 5-11**.

The people God has changed

The section opens in **verse 1** with what it usually taken as a rhetorical question expecting the answer "no", on the assumption that commending ourselves is always bad. However, it is highly probable that Paul is saying something slightly different.

In his letters, and perhaps here in 2 Corinthians above all others, Paul has a highly nuanced attitude to self-commendation. As we have already seen, Paul has no problem in defending himself, backing himself and even *boasting*—when it is clear that his boasting flows from what God has done in us and for us through the Lord Jesus Christ. So boasting is fine when it is boasting about Christ. Self-defence is fine when it is really standing for the gospel. For Paul, even self-commendation is ok, if it is based on the fact that God himself has commissioned us, as in 2:17. It's useful to know that in the first century, self-commendation was entirely appropriate when trying to sort out a relational issue. The final piece of evidence is that the grammar of the sentence is most naturally read as a question expecting the answer "yes"—which gives verse 1 the sense of *Am I commending myself? You bet I am!*

I suspect that as he writes this, Paul feels pretty much like every Christian who ever has to write a CV or a resumé. It's a weird experience: *Here is everything I have achieved. Here is how fantastic I am. But please give me this job because I am humble, servant-hearted and completely dependent on Christ for my sufficiency!* But Paul has deliberately adopted this approach, commending himself because he is a servant of Christ, and he knows that the Corinthians *really need to believe him and stick with him*, as he points them to Christ in the gospel. He would really much rather simply point straight to what God has done as the vindication of his ministry, because he knows that God changes people through the gospel. But desperate times call for desperate measures.

> The lasting fruit of our lives will be people.

So he says, *Yes, I'm commending myself. Or, would you like me to add some letters of recommendation to you, or from you?* Presumably, every Tom, Dick and Socrates who showed up on the philosophy circuit had references proclaiming their genius. Paul would prefer to go down a different route: in **3:2**, he says that the Corinthians themselves are the only credentials that he needs. Paul knows that people matter to God, and people matter to him. That's why he describes God as having inscribed this letter of recommendation on his heart and on those of his team. It's a graphic picture. And it's a striking reminder that authentic ministry is about people.

The lasting fruit of our lives will be people—people whom God has changed through the gospel, spoken by us and our brothers and sisters. For Paul, that included the Corinthians. Even with all the grief they caused him, he describes them in **verse 3** as "a letter from Christ delivered by us, written not with ink but with the Spirit of the living God". Christ wrote the letter, and Paul got to deliver it. To be strictly accurate, Paul could have said that God wrote on the Corinthians' hearts through the gospel which Paul delivered, but you get the point. Paul also highlights that what God has done in them (through his preaching) far outstrips even the definitive moment in the history of the nation of Israel at Mount Sinai ("not on tablets of stone but on tablets of human hearts"): an idea which he will develop over the next few chapters.

For Paul, the primary reason why the Corinthians should continue to listen to him and submit to the gospel is the fact that in the past God used his word—proclaimed through Paul, a flawed messenger—to bring people in Corinth, and the church itself, to life. Paul only has authority because God himself has devolved this authority to him through the gospel. It is God who changes people through the gospel. He does the heavy lifting. He makes the difference. And that takes all the pressure off us, and also refocuses us on *people,* even if those people are making life difficult for us!

Think for a moment about those people with whom you have shared your life and the gospel over the years. Thank God for those whom God has changed and is enabling to keep going. Then pause for a second and think, "Who am I investing in right now?" It's important to ensure that we are regularly asking God to change people through the gospel as we (and others) speak to them in the months and years ahead. All this matters because it really is all about people—people whom God changes through the gospel.

The ministry God has given us

It's because God changes people that Paul can write in **verse 4** that "such is the confidence that we have through Christ towards God". Christ has called Paul, sent Paul and enabled Paul, and because of Christ, Paul can be confident of God's approval. It is God who underwrites everything he does, which brings Paul back to the subject of our "sufficiency" in **verses 5 and 6**.

The word "sufficiency" or "adequacy" is central to Paul's argument in these opening chapters of 2 Corinthians; for Paul, our qualification as God's co-workers is based entirely on God himself as the One who makes the inadequate adequate. There is nothing to trust in or about ourselves. But God has done all that it takes and more to make us "sufficient"—and what has he done? **Verse 6** unlocks everything that Paul says in the rest of this chapter. His basic point is that our adequacy comes from the fact that God has equipped and appointed us as "ministers [or perhaps emissaries] of a new covenant": that is, a covenant under which God actually changes people.

The contrast Paul is working with is a relatively simple one—God worked through Moses back on Mount Sinai, and that was great; but now God has, through Christ, made us sufficient to be ministers of a new covenant. New-covenant ministry is from, by and with the Spirit, rather than with the letter—it brings life rather than death.

Paul isn't writing a theological treatise on the role of the law versus the role of the Spirit here—he is addressing the question of how we can have a realistic view of ourselves and yet get on with ministry without being crippled by doubt or guilt. And his answer? We can get on with it because God has given us a "New-covenant" ministry, which is centred on the fact that God speaks through the message of Jesus' death and resurrection to bring people to new life.

Verses 7-8 are a classic "from the lesser to the greater" argument. Moses' ministry on Sinai was pretty impressive, with smoke and fire and earthquakes, but the proclamation of the word of the gospel in the power of the Spirit leaves it standing! Moses' radiant preaching from behind a veil, detailed in Exodus 34:29-35, was remarkable, but it couldn't actually bring about deep change in anyone. In fact, even while he was on Sinai, 3000 people died as a direct result of their disobedience. But the ministry of the gospel is at a completely different level.

Paul even goes so far in 2 Corinthians 3:7 as to call Moses' ministry "the ministry of death", even though it came "with such glory that the Israelites could not gaze at Moses' face". The inherent weakness of this Mosaic ministry is that it was impermanent—fading. The specific wording says it "was being brought to an end" (the word means "made inoperative", probably by the veil Moses was wearing), unlike the ministry of the Spirit, which, by implication, exceeds it in both quality and endurance.

Paul is very clear that old-covenant ministry was a good thing, in that it reflected something of the glory of God; but new-covenant ministry brings righteousness—real-time, actual, God-honouring, moral righteousness. Our ministry brings real change. It so far outstrips old-covenant ministry that Paul can say in **verses 10-11**:

> "Indeed, in this case, what once had glory [probably referring to Moses' face!] has come to have no glory at all, because of the glory that surpasses it. For if what was [rendered inoperative— Moses' shining face] came with glory, much more will what is permanent have glory."

One light bulb on its own looks bright, but set beside stadium floodlights, it is completely overwhelmed. Such is the difference between what happened on Sinai and the ministry which God has given to us.

So Paul says that we can hold our heads up and get on with gospel ministry because God himself has given us a ministry which is mind-blowingly superior even to that of Moses. Our ministry is wider, deeper and more effective than that of Moses, because God changes people *permanently* through the gospel. This is how he works. This is the

> Our ministry is wider, deeper and more effective than that of Moses, because God changes people permanently through the gospel.

new-covenant ministry to which God has called us—and this is the second reason why we can set ourselves up to keep serving Jesus for the long haul. Not only does God speak through us when we speak the gospel, but he changes people through the gospel. And the third reason to keep going? You can see that in 3:11-18—it's because God reveals his glory through the gospel.

Reason 3: Because God reveals his glory through the gospel

How do we know that we are up to this long-haul ministry? Paul explains in **verse 12**, "Since we have such a hope, we are very bold". Because we have this hope—the solid hope that God has changed us and will change us through the gospel, we keep speaking—and we do so frankly and openly without any veil to stop people seeing the reflected glory of God (as in Acts 28:31).

2 Corinthians **3:13** is a little tricky, but Paul's argument is clear enough: our ministry is not like that of Moses, who put on a veil, literally, so that the Israelites might not gaze at the completion or the fulfilment of what was being made inoperative. The function of Moses' veil was to prevent people from seeing not just Moses' own face but the glory of God, which made his face glow. This ministry could not produce the desired end result—it could not reveal God's glory to people. Instead, the result was that "their minds were hardened". Despite all the positive things we could say about Moses' ministry, it *always* produced this result. Instead of God being glorified as people were changed and came to enjoy the immediate experience of the glory of God, they got nothing. In fact, in the end, it just hardened people.

The remarkable thing is that even today, this is what plays out when the Old Testament is read without reference to Jesus (**verses 14-16**). The veil of blindness to the glory of God is still in place because "only through Christ is it taken away [made inoperative]". Paul even repeats his point to make sure the Corinthians have grasped this. When the gospel is preached, God works to reveal his glory to people like us in a way that would have blown even Moses' mind! Back in the Exodus narratives, the veil meant the glory shining from Moses' face didn't have any effect—now the veil is rendered useless, and we get to gaze on the splendour and majesty of God himself in the Lord Jesus Christ.

"Glory" is a small word which carries huge significance; it is all the "Godness" of God packed into two syllables. The ministry which God gives to us is one in which Christians get to see the glory of the Father in the face of the Son through the Spirit. And that's exactly what Paul says in the last two verses of the chapter.

When Paul says in 2 Corinthians **3:17** that the Lord is the Spirit, he is almost certainly alluding to Exodus 32, as he argues that it was actually God the Spirit who was doing the revealing at Sinai, because it's the Spirit who clears the way for people to see God's glory—so that "where the Spirit of the Lord is, there is freedom". In these new-covenant days, it is the Spirit who removes veils. In 2 Corinthians **3:18** Paul makes this explicit:

"And we all, with unveiled face, beholding the glory of the Lord, are being transformed into the same image from one degree of glory to another."

We get to see God in all his glory in Christ through the Spirit.

What Paul says here about our ministry is staggering. First, God reveals his glory in Christ through the gospel. When Christ

> We should keep going because the ministry which God has given us reveals the glory of God in the face of Christ.

is preached, God works by the Spirit to show people how stunningly, gloriously beautiful Christ is. We should keep going because the ministry which God has given us reveals the glory of God in the face of Christ, and there is no greater beauty, no greater privilege, no greater experience for human beings than this.

Thomas Goodwin, the English Puritan once wrote these words:

"Is Christ so glorious? What will heaven be but the seeing of the glory of Christ? If God had created worlds of glorious creatures, they could never have expressed his glory as his Son [does] ... Wherein lies that great communion of glory that shall be in heaven? It is in seeing the glory of Christ, who is the image of the invisible God that is worshipped ... It is therefore the seeing of Christ that makes heaven; wherefore one said, If I were cast into any hole, if I could have but a cranny to see Christ always, it would be heaven enough..."

(*The Works of Thomas Goodwin,* volume 5, p 548)

When we speak the gospel, when we teach the Bible, when we preach—we need to realise that this is what's going on. God is revealing himself in Christ—and that should be more than enough to re-energise us, sober us and excite us, whether we are struggling to get seven unruly kids to engage with God's word, or stumbling our way through a home Bible-study group on a bad night, or standing in front of God's gathered people. This is what's happening: God is revealing himself through the gospel. And as he does that, he is also transforming us as we observe him at work.

According to Paul, as we gaze at Christ, we become like him, until that day when we shall be like him and shall see him as he is. Now at one level, I wish I could change my physical appearance and character just by staring really hard at someone with more hair, a smaller nose and ears, and with more gifts and fewer character faults, but, sadly, it doesn't work like that—unless we are gazing at the Lord Jesus Christ himself in all his glory. When we stare at him, he rubs off on us. To use Paul's phrase, we are transformed gradually but dramatically "from one degree of glory to another". The phrase could mean that—denoting a process of slow

> As we gaze at Christ, we become like him, until that day when we shall be like him and shall see him as he is.

and gradual transformation, or it could refer to the way in which, like Moses, we are changed by staring at the glory of God. Either way, through the ministry which God has given us, God reveals his glory to us and changes us through exposure to this glory.

Are you worthy?

So, hands up: which of us is worthy to share in a ministry like this? A ministry which involves the God of the universe speaking to people through the gospel, changing people through the gospel, and revealing his glory through the gospel in a way which remakes us in the image of Christ. Who is sufficient for a new-covenant ministry like this? Our natural reaction will be to say "not me". But we would be wrong. Verses 5-6 say this plainly.

And if God has spoken, who are we to argue? So in our weakness, our insecurity, our hypocrisy, our brokenness, we just need to get on with it and take this life-giving, glory-revealing, heart-changing gospel to a world which desperately needs it, in the strength which our God supplies, for the glory of the Lord Jesus.

Questions for reflection

1. Do you really expect God to change people you know and love through the gospel? What does this passage say to you about that?

2. God has given us a greater ministry than that of Moses. Do you believe that? If that's true, what difference does that make?

3. What can we expect God to do in us and through us through the gospel? Is that reflected in the way in which we live together as God's people?

4. LIFE AS A PLASTIC BAG

You may not realise this, but before the 1980s, most TV shows were, how can I put it—completely unrealistic. Cop shows, in particular, generally involved scenic locations—often Hawaii—and handsome detectives who chased dastardly criminals, exchanging hundreds of bullets before slapping on the cuffs, without anyone being hurt.

Then came *Hill Street Blues*.

CNN once called it "the most influential TV show ever". Suddenly the words "gritty" and "realistic" entered the vocabulary of TV. Every show in this ground-breaking drama started with the morning briefing in Hill Street Police Station, in a city centre somewhere in America. As the boys in blue hit the mean streets, the sergeant would say, "Let's be careful out there". That's what it feels like to be part of God's kingdom project in our world. In particular, that's what it feels like to be in leadership in the church.

We've already seen that when it comes to the churches that he has planted or spent time with (like that in Corinth), *Paul cares*. In 11:28, he will speak of "the daily pressure on me of my anxiety for all the churches". *He cares*. That's the way it should be both with leaders and with every member of the body of Christ—because we live in a difficult, broken world, and the stakes are high when it comes to living for Jesus.

Jesus himself said he was sending his followers out "as sheep among wolves", and it's perfectly natural to be concerned that no one gets eaten! Our great prayer for each other should be that together we would

This chapter is all about the secret of long-term, self-denying, Christ-honouring life ministry.

so shaped and mastered by the gospel that we will be, in the grace of God, set up for a lifetime of serving Jesus in all kinds of gospel ministry, or, to use the little phrase that controls this chapter, that we will "not lose heart".

As we have seen over the first three chapters of this letter, Paul is engaged in a battle for the hearts and minds of the Corinthian church, which he himself has been involved in planting. They have been wavering in their commitment to him and to the gospel. So in chapter 1 he reminds them that God himself stands behind all gospel ministry. Then in chapter 2 Paul pushes them to follow him, because he is just imitating Christ. And then in chapter 3 Paul insists that God has made *all* of us competent to exercise a new-covenant, Spirit-driven, life-shaping ministry through the gospel.

Lurking in the background of all this, of course, was the Corinthian tendency to value everything that sounded impressive and turned over a quick buck. One more problem with the passing philosophy roadshows which caused such chaos in the Corinthian church was that these philosophers didn't stick around to see the effects of their fine-sounding words. They came, they got paid, and they went, leaving other people to clean up the mayhem they left in their wake. But not Paul: he was in this for the long haul. His long relationship with the Corinthians (including multiple visits and letters) was already ample evidence of that.

And Paul desperately wants the Corinthians to understand what he's on about, because he knows that only the gospel can equip us for and sustain us in a lifetime of ministry. As he says in 4:1 and again in verse 16, this is a matter of *not losing heart*. Chapter 4 is all about the secret of long-term, self-denying, Christ-honouring life ministry. Paul lays it all out—here is his worldview, his philosophy of ministry and his heart attitude. This is what it will take to last the pace in a hostile world.

In 2 Corinthians 4, Paul lays out eight principles which will set us up to keep going in gospel ministry without either giving up or losing heart. This is Paul at his most passionate; this is Paul at his most revealing. Here is Paul on the reality of gospel ministry. Here is all that Paul has learned about keeping going in gospel-driven ministry, condensed into one chapter.

Principle 1: God has shown us mercy in giving us this ministry

The great thing is that, as **verse 1** shows, we get to share in God's work in our world—we have this ministry by the mercy of God, and so "we do not lose heart". By the word "ministry", Paul is referring to everything we were looking at in 2:14-3:18: the life-giving, new-covenant, glory-revealing, character-transforming ministry of the Spirit through the gospel. And Paul insists that God has given all of us a part in this ministry simply because he is immeasurably kind. Paul keeps going as a Christian because he knows that God has brought him into his family and involved him in the work of the kingdom for his good. This is the mercy of God in operation. And this is why Paul has absolutely no intention of giving up: because he knows that his ministry—no matter how hard—is good for him, because he has been given this opportunity by the mercy of God—the kindness that God showed him when he really deserved the opposite.

Even this first phrase will have a massively transformative effect on our thinking, and eventually on our entire life with and service of Christ. The "ministry" we have—which, as we saw in chapter 3, is speaking the gospel in the power of the Spirit, whatever our role, wherever we get to do it—is a dramatic expression of the same mercy that God has shown us in the death, resurrection and rule of the Lord Jesus Christ.

I am sitting at my desk in Brisbane, Australia, writing this because of the mercy of God to me. You are doing what you do by the mercy of God. You go to work in the morning to interact with all kinds of people who aren't yet Christians by the mercy of God; you help with the kids and youth ministry in church by the mercy of God; you got the chance to speak the gospel into someone's life yesterday by the mercy of God, and so it goes on. We have these opportunities *by the mercy of God.*

God has involved us in his work in our world for his glory—*and for our good.* That means we really shouldn't whinge because, even if we think this is a nightmare, it's good for us. It means we shouldn't be scared or bothered by people, but it is God in his kindness who has involved us in new-covenant ministry—so we should get on with it, speaking the truth of the gospel lovingly to everyone we can and, as Paul says in **4:2**, doing it with transparency and integrity. No tricks, no manipulation, no deceit, no twisting the message to suit ourselves or other people—just "the open statement of the truth".

This is so very important. Because we are in this "because of God's mercy", we don't do what Paul, in effect, calls *sneaky ministry*—he spells out exactly what he means using three phrases: (i) no rhetorical tricks, (ii) no twisting of the message (he uses a word which originally meant "fish bait"); (iii) just an open statement of the truth. We are to preach, tell and explain the gospel in a pattern of speaking and living which is commendable to every possible variety of human conscience hearing the gospel—because we are serving in the sight of the God who has shown us mercy. Our ministry—whatever it may be—comes from him, is done in his full view and will ultimately be assessed by him. That's the first principle of ministry which will guard us against losing heart.

Principle 2: We are in a fight—so of course it's going to be hard

One of the criticisms of Paul that seemed to have gained some traction with the Corinthians was that *his* message, unlike those of the passing philosophical hucksters, lacked a certain popular appeal. *Some people just don't get your preaching, Paul.* That can't have been easy to hear, but Paul doesn't take it personally. In fact, he sees right to the heart of the spiritual issue, and articulates a principle which is absolutely vital for every Christian to grasp, in **verse 3**: "And even if our gospel is veiled [like Moses' face, and therefore ineffective in revealing God's glory to people], it is veiled among those who are perishing"—that is, those who are facing divine judgment. The issue is not with the message, but with the people. As Charles Hodge, a 19th-century American theologian pointed out, "The sun does not cease to be the sun although the blind do not see it". And why are people unable to see God's glory in the gospel? Paul explains in **verse 4**—it's down to the "god of this world". It's because we are in a spiritual battle, which means we have a real live enemy.

This is the only place in Scripture where the noun *theos* ("God" or "god") is applied to Satan, the evil one—but immediately it is made clear that his influence is limited to "this world" or "this age", in contrast to the universal reign of God. And what has Satan done? He has managed to do what the veil on Moses' face did back on Sinai—he has prevented the light which emanates from the gospel—as Christ's glory itself is revealed by it—doing its transforming work on people. Christ's glory shines through the gospel bringing light and truth—the evil one does his damnedest to keep people in the dark. And we really do need to know this.

Of course, it's important to grasp the fact that we can't bring dead people to life—only God can do that through the gospel by the Spirit. But that isn't the whole picture. There are also powers at work who are actively opposing our efforts to bring the light of the glory of Christ to people as we share the gospel. So are you up for a fight? Knowing up front that we are going to get one should set us up better for the long haul.

> We can't bring dead people to life—only God can do that through the gospel by the Spirit.

Principle 3: It's not about us

It's worth quoting **verse 5** in full:

> "For what we proclaim is not ourselves, but Jesus Christ as Lord,
> with ourselves as your servants for Jesus' sake."

In his commentary on 2 Corinthians, C.K. Barrett says, "It would be hard to describe the Christian ministry more comprehensively in so few words", and I think he's right. We don't proclaim ourselves "but Jesus Christ as Lord".

> Paul refused to talk about himself, other than to say he was their slave for the sake of Jesus.

I'm not sure that the Corinthians would have been quite so enthusiastic about Paul's slogan, at least at first. The Corinthians had a strong **elitist** tendency. They liked their **orators** to be educated at the best private schools and top universities. Being big-headed was an advantage. But Paul refused to talk about himself, other than to say he was their slave for the sake of Jesus. As Calvin said succinctly:

> "The man who wishes to preach only Christ must forget himself ...
> Here all pastors of the church are reminded of their rank and con-
> dition, for whatever title of honour they may have to distinguish
> them, they are nothing more than the servants of believers, for the
> only way to serve Christ is by serving his church as well."

> (John Calvin, *Commentary on 2nd Corinthians*, p 56)

All this and more flows from the fact that "Jesus Christ is Lord"—those four words which comprise the most profound and yet simplest of all Christian confessions. Murray Harris says that wrapped up in these four words there are at least eight implications:

- Jesus of Nazareth is the Christ.

- Jesus Christ is God.

- He has supremacy over all things.

- Christ therefore triumphed over death and all powers through his death and resurrection.

- All people are accountable to him.

- Anyone who grasps this has grasped the Christian message.

- Anyone who says this has made a personal declaration of faith.

- Believing this repudiates all other allegiances.

Which just underlines what Paul says in the first half of verse 5—it's not about us; it's about *him*.

A basic step in a lifetime of gospel ministry is to get over ourselves: to realise that ultimately whether people like us or not doesn't really matter. Whether we are perceived as successful or not doesn't matter. Whether we are recognised or not doesn't matter. All that matters is preaching Christ as Lord. We keep going because it's about him, not us.

Principle 4: God has shown us his glory in the face of Christ

In **verse 6**, Paul, alluding to Genesis 1:3 or Isaiah 9:2 (or possibly both), spells out that God has shone a light into our darkness "to give the light of the knowledge of the glory of God in the face of Jesus Christ". But whether the first part of the verse is referring to creation or redemption, it is quite clear that, in Christ, God has turned back to us, allowing us to gaze at his glory in unprecedented ways, as we see the face of Christ in the gospel.

I have been following Christ for my entire adult life. When have the really sweet and effective seasons been? When I have seen and savoured Christ himself most richly in the gospel. It's not exactly a stunning revelation, I know, but the more I gaze at Jesus in the gospel, the more transfixed I am with Jesus in his death and resurrection, the more single-minded and determined and unflinching and focused I am on gospel ministry, the more entranced I am with Jesus in his glory, the less likely I am to lose heart. Here's what John Piper so helpfully says on 2 Corinthians 4:6:

> "This is the highest and best and final good that makes all the other good things promised in the gospel good. Justification is good news because it makes us stand accepted by the one whose glory we want to see and savour above all things. Forgiveness is good news because it cancels all the sins that keep me from seeing and enjoying the glory of Christ who is the image of God. Removal of wrath and salvation from hell are good news because now in my escape from eternal misery I find eternal pleasure beholding the glory of God in the face of Christ. Eternal life is good news because this is eternal life, Jesus said, that they know me and him who sent me. And freedom from pain and sickness and conflict are good news because, in my freedom from pain, I am no longer distracted from the fullest enjoyment of the glory of Christ who is the image of God."
>
> (*Brothers, We Are Not Professionals,* p 57-58)

That's the fourth principle which gives people like us every reason to keep going.

Questions for reflection

1. When was the last time you thanked God for his kindness to you in setting up your life the way it is just now? Spend some time doing that now.

2. What difference does the fact that we are "in a fight" make to the way in which we think? Pray? Do evangelism? Approach issues in church?

3. Why are we so prone to taking things personally? What can we do about that?

PART TWO

We are halfway through Paul's eight-point list of principles that give people like us a reason not to lose heart.

Principle 5: Our weakness is part of God's strategy

This section begins with this famous statement in **verse 7**:

"But we have this treasure in jars of clay, to show that the surpassing power belongs to God and not to us."

I am struggling to think of a statement in the Bible which is more precious to me just now than this. For I am feeling my age.

Last Friday, my over-35s football team (I should say most of us qualify with plenty of room to spare) played our first pre-season friendly. I have been training pretty hard over the summer, so I am in better condition than I have been for almost 20 years. However, that is not saying much. On Sunday morning, I gamely went out for a run as part of my recovery process. All I can say is that I am glad none of you were close to my house at 7am last Sunday morning. Every step was pain. The game had been fine—I played in midfield and covered a lot of ground for an old bloke. But the recovery? Every season it takes longer and is more painful than the one before.

I am gradually coming to terms with the fact that this terracotta pot, this ancient supermarket plastic bag, this disposable, breakable, dispensable jar of clay is cracking in more places than I can count. But according to Paul, *that's the point!* Our weakness is actually part of God's strategy. It isn't that God didn't realise that we would be so hopeless. It isn't that God didn't have any choice—he deliberately decided to set things up in such a way that he works in our weakness.

The treasure of gazing at the glory of God in Christ with unveiled faces is transported in disposable, affordable, unexceptional pots— and God set it up like this on purpose and for a purpose: to show that the surpassing power belongs to God, not to us. *Our weakness* is part of God's strategy to display his glory to a watching world. It's supposed to be like this. And once we realise this, it enables us to keep going without being flattened.

Verses 8 and 9 explain how this works—we face all kinds of pain but aren't *crushed,* all kinds of challenges but aren't *driven to despair,* all kinds of opposition but aren't *forsaken* by God; we may even be *struck down, but* we won't be *destroyed.* Our suffering provides the platform for the display of God's power. God will display his glory through us, and how will this happen? In the context of pain, struggle, difficulty, discouragement and suffering—this is how it is for disposable plastic bags. If all this weren't enough, Paul hammers it home in **verse 10**—there are no exceptions. This life is for all of us, all the time; we are all "carrying in the body the death of Jesus, so that the life of Jesus" might be displayed in us.

> Our suffering provides the platform for the display of God's power.

The word for death here is a highly unusual one, and it refers not to Jesus' death on the cross but his long journey through suffering up to and including the cross. Paul is saying that our weakness and suffering are the essential and enduring characteristics of ministry—so if we are intending to serve Jesus for the long haul, we'd better get our heads around this now, because God uses weak people—terracotta pots, plastic bags—to bring the light of the gospel of the glory of Christ to people. **Verse 11** makes it plain that this is the way it's going to be, for this is the way that Jesus reveals his glory in our world. This is the cost of gospel proclamation. Paul sums it up bluntly in **verse 12**: "So death is at work in us, but life in you".

Do you want a sentence to carry around in the front of your Bible or in your wallet, or to write above your desk that will keep things in perspective and keep you on track in the years ahead? Try this for size—"Death is at work in us, but life in you". We are not immortal.

We aren't even strong. And we take the gospel as men and women who are dying to men and women who are dying.

If we truly understand this, we will not lose heart but give ourselves to sharing the gospel with others while we have breath.

Principle 6: The Bible tells us it will be tough to keep going

This is no surprise to Paul. So how and why does he stick at it? Because the Bible tells him to. That is why Paul quotes the Old Testament in **verse 13**: "I believed, and so I spoke", and he goes on to say, "We also believe, and so we also speak". To be honest, Paul could have picked almost any part of the Old Testament to make his point for the theme of suffering in the service of God is *everywhere*. But he chose to quote from Psalm 116:10. The psalmist knew that suffering is real, that opposition is real, and that death is real; and he speaks honestly about the reality of his experience: *I am greatly afflicted, and everyone is lying about me.* But he also speaks the gospel, as he takes hold of the cup of salvation and calls on the name of the Lord in the hearing of everyone. Paul's point is this: every time he picks up his Bible, it reminds him that he can expect to suffer as he serves the Lord. Having realistic biblical expectations is a great help when it comes to keeping going!

In 2000 my wife, Fiona, and I moved to Dublin, where I became the pastor of a pair of Presbyterian churches which had no evangelical tradition. The early years were interesting to say the least. During that challenging period, I used to get a regular email from an old friend in Sydney, John Chapman, which contained only 15 words: "Dear Gazza, please remember they crucified the Lord Jesus—why should you expect anything better?" The Bible tells us it will be tough to keep going—and knowing that is a real help.

Principle 7: We will be raised with Christ

Part of the problem with living where I do in Queensland, Australia (the Sunshine State) is that life here is *just too nice.* Our tourist slogan is remarkably accurate—it generally is "beautiful one day, perfect the next". Three or four weeks of heightened humidity is as tough as it gets. The problem with this is that it lulls Queenslanders into a false sense of security. We don't want anything better than this—just what we've got with a slightly cooler breeze. The unfortunate side effect of living in a beautiful place with perfect weather is that we're not looking forward to anything. Paul's experience of life could hardly have been more different. He was constantly being chased, beaten up and ac-cused. But because of that, the hope which he describes in **4:14**—that the God "who raised the Lord Jesus will raise us also with Jesus and bring us with you into his presence"—was an enormous incentive to keep going.

> To be a real Christian, for Paul, is to keep going to the very end, knowing that a glorious future is guaranteed for us.

This is a key feature of Paul's writings. According to Paul, the general resurrection (that is, *ours*) has been anticipated and initiated by *Christ's* resurrection. He dealt with this at some length in 1 Corinthians 15 and now returns to it, to underline for the Corinthians that it is always worth hanging on to the end. To be a real Christian, for Paul, is to keep going to the very end, knowing that a glorious future is guaranteed for us.

Since I was five, my life has been punctuated by travelling to watch Northern Ireland play international soccer matches in Belfast. I generally went with my dad and my brother. And at almost every game, my dad suggested leaving early to beat the traffic. It drove me nuts. I am a "to the bitter end" kind of guy—no matter how slim the chances, no matter how dire the situation, I always clung onto the hope of a last-minute revival, even when we were three goals down. In this passage, Paul holds out more than the faintest glimmer of hope of a last-minute turnaround. Paul says we have every reason to hang in there to the end, because the end will bring the most stunning reversal in fortunes, as we are raised together to delight in Christ's presence.

The final basic principle that gives us an incentive to keep going sums up the first seven…

Principle 8: God is working for our good and his glory

In **verse 15**, Paul's summary statement runs like this: "For it is all for your sake, so that as grace extends to more and more people it may increase thanksgiving, to the glory of God". Everything Paul does—in fact everything we all do as ministers of the new covenant—will result in more and more people discovering the grace of God, giving thanks to God, bringing us more and more joy, and resulting in the glory of God. This is what's happening in us and through us. This is what enables people like you and me to keep pressing on—because we know that God is at work through the gospel for our good and his glory.

It is this conviction that stands behind this extraordinary statement written by the 17th-century scientist and theologian Blaise Pascal:

"I ask you neither for health nor for sickness, for life nor death; but that you may dispose of my health and sickness, my life and my death, for your glory … You alone know what is expedient for me; you are the sovereign master, do with me according to your will. Give to me or take away from me, only conform my will to yours. I know but one thing, Lord, that it is good for me to follow you and bad to offend you. Apart from that, I know not what is good or bad in anything. I know not which is most profitable to me, health or sickness, wealth or poverty, nor anything else in the world. That discernment is beyond the power of men or angels, and is hidden among the secrets of your providence, which I adore, but do not seek to fathom."

(For the full prayer, see *Pensées*, p 370-378)

Trusting the God who works for our good and his glory is Paul's final reason to keep going. No wonder he says in verse 16 "so we do not lose heart".

Why we should not lose heart

In many ways, this is a very unusual passage for Paul. He has thrown the theological kitchen sink at the Corinthians in one final impassioned attempt to push them over the line into gospel faithfulness. His approach in 2 Corinthians 4 is less one of careful theological persuasion and more of going in with all guns blazing and with every conceivable reason he can think of to keep pressing on. And in verses 16-18, he has one more go.

He reminds the Corinthians that there is every reason "not to lose heart" (**v 16**) Even though he is facing all kinds of challenges and opposition, and even though his body is creaking, everything he goes through every day is contributing to God's great renewal project, which he has been describing in the preceding verses. What's going on externally, as attested by the wrinkles, scars and general degradation of his body, only partly hides the glorious renewal project that God is conducting moment by moment on the inside.

In **verse 17**, Paul adds that the pain of going through all this pales into insignificance when it is measured against what it's achieving. He describes the trouble as "light" and "fleeting", but it produces an eternal tonnage of glory in a way that just blows his mind, as God himself shares his unimaginable riches and grandeur with us.

According to **verse 18**, then, grasping all this will completely re-orient the way in which we look at the world. We'll have a growth mindset, an unshakeable optimism and a clear grasp on reality as we serve Christ for the rest of our lives. We'll have a growth mindset because even though "everything to do with this present life and world" is wasting away, the gospel is changing us, remaking us in the likeness of Jesus himself.

We'll have an unshakeable optimism because "this light momentary affliction is preparing for us an eternal weight of glory beyond all comparison". In his book *Future Grace,* John Piper comments:

"This means that the decaying of his body was not meaningless. The pain and pressure and frustration were not happening in vain. They were not vanishing into a black hole of pointless suffering. Instead this suffering was producing for him an eternal weight of glory far beyond all comparison ... When he is hurting he fixes his eyes not on how heavy the hurt is, but on how heavy the glory will be because of the hurt."
(p 359-360)

> You have signed up for suffering, disruption and abuse; for frustration, lack of appreciation and disappointment. But every second will be worth it.

And we'll have a clear grasp on reality as we pay special attention not to the things that are seen "but to the things that are unseen. For the things that are seen are transient, but the things that are unseen are eternal". Throwing yourself into gospel ministry is hard. I'd be lying to you if I said anything else. You have signed up for suffering, disruption and abuse; for frustration, lack of appreciation and disappointment. But you know what? Every second of it will be worth it—because God is at work for your good and his glory. We need not lose heart because we are being changed, because we are storing up an eternal tonnage of glory. We are spending our lives on the one thing that really matters. So brothers and sisters—*do not lose heart!*

Questions for reflection

1. Why is our weakness not something to be ashamed of?

2. What makes keeping going so hard on the one hand and so important on the other?

3. What is God doing in us and in our world? Why is that a motivating factor to keep pressing on?

5. SEEING THROUGH THE GOSPEL?

If I had to pick one word to sum up 2 Corinthians so far, do you know what it would be? *Intense.* Reading this letter is like walking into a room where two people who clearly know each other well and seem to love each other deeply are having a very full-on conversation. They could be, say, a married couple. And they could even be having what you might describe as a fight. Hard to imagine but do your best.

As we stand listening, slightly awkwardly, wondering if we should stay or go, some things are very obvious: they have some serious issues; they have a lot of shared history, which we don't know much about; and they clearly know how to push each other's buttons. Now it's also clear that things are heating up—and getting to a point where either this couple are going to kiss and make up, or things are about to blow up. Time for a discreet exit to the kitchen to make a cup of tea perhaps—or perhaps we should stick around and see exactly how this plays out…

Paul has so far laid out patiently that *all* ministry, including his own, is ultimately God's work. He has carefully reminded the Corinthians of his own trustworthiness and love for them. He has underlined that God speaks and works (revealing his glory) through the proclamation of the gospel, and by no other means. In the previous chapter we saw that Paul gently explained how God himself has given us all the resources we need to keep going with this kind of ministry for the long haul. And now, in chapter 5, he gets to the sharp end of his argument.

Remember, unlike in most of his other letters, Paul is writing to try to win the Corinthians over—or more likely back—to the cause of Christ. He has spent years with them, patiently teaching them face to face. This isn't Romans, where he carefully and logically introduces his gospel step by theological step. This is 2 Corinthians, where Paul's purpose is less to explain and more to persuade, appeal and urge—and in chapter 5, Paul is pushing really hard to get the Corinthians to buy into four very un-Corinthian things.

> To be a Corinthian was to live for the moment. To be a Corinthian was to talk yourself up.

To be a Corinthian was to live for the moment. To be a Corinthian was to talk yourself up. To be a Corinthian was to be impressed by a good education, a good brain and good speech. To be a Corinthian was to switch political and religious allegiance every time the wind changed. And Paul is writing to remind them that, now that they belong to Christ, all that should fade away. Which is why, in an increasingly desperate attempt to get them to side with him and the gospel, Paul lays out four very un-Corinthian characteristics which mark people who belong to Christ. That they also happen to be deeply countercultural for most of us too means that this chapter packs a powerful punch, both then and now.

The first very un-Corinthian trait which marks out authentic gospel ministry dominates the first ten verses of 2 Corinthians 5.

We look to the future

Paul had already written at some length to the Corinthians about the future—and in particular, the resurrection of the body (in both 1 Corinthians 15, and, as we saw in the previous chapter, in 2 Corinthians 4:18-20). But now he picks up where he left off, by talking once more about the resurrection body that awaits us, and the delightful, tantalising prospect of being with Jesus Christ for ever.

Before we get into the details, let's make sure we are clear on just how important this is. The resurrection hope is one of *the* defining features of Christianity, and yet we let it slip offstage so easily. For those of us who live comfortably in rich nations, life is so good that there is little need for hope, that's as easy as it was back in Corinth.

Many of us in the prosperous, English-speaking world will spend most of our lives surrounded by people for whom life is *so* good that hope is a luxury we don't have much need for. The Australian social commentator Mark McCrindle describes the 18-year-olds of 2020 like this:

> "The youth of 2020 are part of the most formally educated gen-eration in history—starting education younger than ever and projected to stay in education for longer than ever. As the chil-dren of older, wealthier parents with fewer siblings and more entertainment and technological options, it is likely that they will be the most entertained and materially endowed generation of children ever."

The challenge is to bring the hope of the gospel to countless people like this, because, as they will discover in due course, real hope won't be found anywhere else.

In **5:1**, Paul starts by tackling our mortality head on. "For we know that if the tent that is our earthly home is destroyed"(which it most certainly will be), then "we have a building from God, a house not made with hands, eternal in the heavens". Paul compares our bodies to a tent, and our resurrection bodies to a permanent home built by God himself, which will last for ever in the new creation.

In the ancient world, it wasn't unusual to compare the body to a tent. The best that people could hope for was release into some kind of disembodied existence free from aches and pains. So in the *Wis-dom of Solomon*, an intertestamental fusion of **Hellenistic** philoso-phy and Jewish **piety**, we read these words:

> "For a corruptible body burdens the soul, and the earthly tent weighs down a world full of cares." (Wisdom of Solomon 9:15)

The writer is looking forward to getting out of his leaky tent! But our hope is far superior to that—life in the tent has its issues, but according to 2 Corinthians **5:2**, "we groan, longing to put on our heavenly dwelling". As you can see, Paul starts to mix his metaphors here, as he compares this heavenly house to a jacket, but the fact that our life after death is going to be so much better is clear.

The ESV for **verse 3**, along with many other translations, says, "if indeed by putting it on we may not be found naked". The sense is something like this: *assuming that if we put on our resurrection body, then we won't be found naked (or underdressed) for the new creation*. It may be an oblique reference to the parable of the wedding guests in Matthew 22, where an inappropriately dressed guest is cast out. Paul's point is either that we don't need to worry that we will be stuck in some intermediate state for ever, or simply that the resurrection is the guarantee that we'll be set up to enjoy life with God for ever in the new heavens and the new earth.

This means that if we are Christians, the only reason we have to complain is because we are looking forward to this so much, rather than because we are feeling the weight of an empty future. It isn't that we want everything to be over—"we groan, being burdened—not that we would be unclothed" (2 Corinthians **5:4**)—but that we can't wait for what's coming, when we will be "further clothed". Instead of fearing oblivion, we are looking forward to the day when "what is mortal may be swallowed up by life". We look to the future because it's going to be great. God himself has already guaranteed this—and has done so decisively. This promise is underwritten by God himself (**v 5**), "who has given us the Spirit as a guarantee". God has already paid the deposit for the new creation. We get to experience the power and presence of God through the Spirit now, in a way that anticipates the full-blown version in the age to come. Paul then builds on this in 5:6-10, and explains how and why this makes a real difference to the way we think and act and relate.

Verse 6 explains that this reality changes our mood and our outlook on all of life: "So we are always of good courage" (perhaps better translated as: "being confident of this"), because we know that what we experience now is a faint shadow of what is to come. Paul says that "while we are at home in the body we are away from the Lord". Life now for some of us is rich and good, but what is to come is better by far. It is this prospect which shapes the way we act and react right now, "for we walk by faith, not by sight" (**v 7**). This

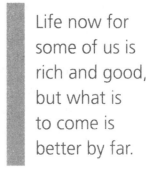

Life now for some of us is rich and good, but what is to come is better by far.

world, this life, is *not* the only thing or even the ultimate expression of our lives, and so we walk in a way which is shaped by what God has revealed, not by what can be seen.

Now that's very easy to say—but what does that mean in practice? I have a sneaking suspicion that the default for many Bible Christians across the world is to live "by sight". To live by sight is to act as if we are in control, to operate on the principle that we can fix things. It is to rely on our own abilities, to act as if position and reputation and appearance matter rather than clinging on by faith to the fact that only the things of the Lord will last!

Last week I realised something deeply shameful about myself, which reminded me of just how easy it is to start to live by sight rather than faith. My mobile phone bill arrived in my inbox. Everyone's phones are on the statement, and as I started to glance through it, my eye was caught by the fact that I have only four more repayments on my handset. Now I have to say that I am completely happy with my phone. It isn't exactly outdated. But one line on my statement was enough to get me thinking "Aaahhh—an upgrade! Rather than paying the phone company less money, I can give them more and get a shiny new phone which will obviously increase my happiness and contentment". It's a tiny example of how living-by-sight thinking can infect our minds at the most mundane and ordinary levels.

But look at what Paul says in **verse 8**: we know that living by sight is the way we will live in the new creation, and we can even say that "we would rather be away from the body and at home with the Lord". He may be speaking of stepping into Christ's presence immediately when we die, or looking forward to the resurrection body; either way, it is *this reality* which dominates his thought processes and decision-making right now—and what's the conclusion? **Verse 9**: "So whether we are at home or away, we make it our aim to please him". Living by faith then is living to please Jesus Christ both now, and in the future, at the tribunal which Paul describes next.

> We need to live *now* in a way that takes into account the fact that our lives will be examined *then.*

The language of **verse 10** is quite arresting. Not only will everyone "appear before the judgment seat of Christ", but the end result is that all of us will "receive what is due for what we have done in the body, whether good or evil". According to Paul, we will all appear before the divine bench, and a judgment will be handed down which is comprehensive—both in its detail and its extent—and individual. There has been much discussion over the years about this verse: who is judged and on what basis? On balance, I think Paul is talking exclusively about Christians here, as we are subject to the kind of evaluation of our lives and ministries that Paul described back in 1 Corinthians 3:10-18. The idea is one of accountability: we need to live *now* in a way that takes into account the fact that our lives will be examined *then*, without slipping into a works-righteousness mindset.

The idea that Christians might be rewarded in some way or suffer loss for their faithful service or lack of it is a hotly contested one. But there are some passages (like 1 Corinthians 3, the Parable of the Talents in Matthew 25:14-30, and 1 Peter 5:4) which do seem to imply that this may be the case.

In his brilliant and delightfully written *Reformed Dogmatics,* Herman Bavinck says:

"If we had done everything we were supposed to do, we would still be 'unworthy slaves' who gave the master more trouble than profit. But now that not even that is the case, now that the most saintly people have only a small beginning of perfect obedience, now that even their best works are defective and impure, and they owe everything they are, own and do as believers to the grace of God, now all notions on their part of a reward, of merit, which would give them a right to reward in the true sense of the word are out of the question. What child of God would have the nerve to let such an idea arise and express it before the judgment seat of God? The situation is very different, however, if God on his part wants to picture the salvation and glory he desires to give his children using the imagery of wages and reward. And that is indeed what he does throughout the scriptures. He does that to spur on, to encourage and to comfort his children, who being his children are already his heirs … The inheritance which is then kept for us in heaven is not a wage paid out to employees in proportion to what they have earned, but a reward that the Father in heaven grants to his children out of sheer grace. That reward is one of the many incentives for moral conduct, but by no means a rule or law, for it arises from God's will alone."

(Volume 4, p 265-66)

So this isn't payback, but it is an incentive for us to live by faith, not by sight, knowing the grace that awaits us. It is God's tender, gentle encouragement to us to live to please him as we follow in the steps of the One who has already defined what a life pleasing to God looks like, and lived that life for us.

I should add one more thing: living to please someone else gets a bad press just now. In the 21st century, our wellbeing is routinely tied to pleasing ourselves. We are urged to focus on our own self-actualisation, and self-affirmation, and a thousand other forms of self-focus.

One of the many problems with this is that it is entirely focused on the present—the Corinthians (like most of us) would have loved it. But not Paul. He urges the Corinthians, and us, to go against our natural grain and look to the future: to live by faith, not by sight.

Questions for reflection

1. Is there any evidence in your life that you have slipped into living for today?

2. Why is hope for the future such a powerful motivator? Does it work like that for you? Why do you think that is? Why is it so important that we proclaim—and live—a gospel of hope in our comfortable world?

3. Does it ever occur to you that God will talk through the details of our lives with us one day? How do you react to that thought?

PART TWO

After the extended discussion of the importance of looking to the future in 2 Corinthians 5:1-10, the second counter-cultural trait of authentic gospel ministry is laid out for us much more briefly in 5:11-13.

We fear God, not people

The overriding principle in this short section is not hard to pick our. **Verse 11** spells it out: "Therefore, knowing the fear of the Lord, we persuade others".

This isn't the first time that Paul has taken up the matter of *people pleasing* with the Corinthians, because it is a big issue for them. Partly because they are human and partly because they live in an atmosphere in which deriving your significance from other people's opinion of you thrives (see, for example, 1 Corinthians 4:3-5). Paul insists that we need to learn to live before an audience of one. We need to fear God, not people.

There is no more pressing issue for anyone who is involved with ministry of any kind at any level in the church of the Lord Jesus. Being enslaved by the opinions of other people brings great pain to us. Nothing will crush us more effectively than the criticism of other people if we haven't embraced this truth. Nothing will puff us up more quickly, or with more toxicity, than the praise of other people if that's what we're living for. This will devastate your heart, compromise your decision-making and ultimately undermine your whole service of the Lord Jesus Christ. And the problem with it is that for almost all of us, it comes so very naturally. Which of us doesn't enjoy

> Nothing will puff us up more quickly, or with more toxicity, than the praise of other people.

praise and recoil from criticism? Which of us would opt for a crushing rebuke rather than a pat on the back? So what are we to do?

Here's what Paul prescribes: *take your stance as an open book before God.* This is the only posture that will free us up to love others, to persuade them of the truth of the gospel, and to speak the gospel into their lives, even if they resent us—even if they think we are crazy. That's what he means in 2 Corinthians **5:11** when he adds, "But what we are is known to God". Paul's own stance before God, his relationship with God, is characterised by simple, straightforward honesty.

> "Here I am, Lord—this is all I've got. I am what I am—and even then, it's only by your grace."

It's so easy to pretend before God, to try to persuade God and ourselves that we are better than we actually are—that we are making more progress, that we are more together, that we are less sinful than we actually are. But that is unbelievably dumb. The only sensible thing for people like us—for people like Paul—is to start and end each day saying "Here I am, Lord—this is all I've got. I am what I am—and even then, it's only by your grace."

In the second half of verse 11, Paul then adds this: "I hope it is known also to your conscience". This sounds as if it might be the last shot Paul has to fire: he appeals to their *conscience*—that slightly unreliable instrument designed to detect when our life does (or doesn't) match up with what God says to us in the gospel. The apostle says, *whatever else you may think of me, you know this much is true—you know it in your spiritual gut: that I don't play games or try to impress because my overwhelming concern is to seek God's approval and no-one else's.* And he longs for them to follow his example in this. That's why he adds the following two verses.

Paul makes clear that he is using himself as an example to encourage them ("giving you cause to boast about us", **v 12**), so that they might reject those who "boast about outward appearance", and instead focus on living to fear and please God. Paul encourages them to take the fight to those who are all about reputation and impressing people—all about presentation rather than content. He even adds *You know what? Even if they think I'm a bit mad, who cares?* In **verse 13** he declares, "For if we are beside ourselves, it is for God; if we are in our right mind, it is for you". The apostle and his companions are living to please God, which frees them up to love the Corinthians.

Fearing people does so much damage to our lives. It stops our evangelism in its tracks, it hamstrings our ability to lead, it stops us saying the hard thing and pushes us into lying, saying things to manipulate people into saying things to make us feel good. But thank God that in Christ we have no need to act like that, because Christ has died and risen, and we are united to him, and so we fear God alone.

We love people because of Christ

It is hard to think of a part of the Bible which contains quite so many key slogans for Christian ministry—in this chapter they just keep coming. In **verse 14**, Paul says that "the love of Christ controls us". The word "control" here includes both the idea of motivation and direction—so "constrains" or "compels" us would perhaps be a better translation. Having met Christ on the Damascus road, having encountered him in the gospel—Paul's way of relating to people could never be the same again. Now, as a follower of Christ, he is forced, compelled, driven to love people as Christ did and does.

That's the conclusion he has reached in v 14. Why? It's because "one has died for all, therefore all have died". And this one death has the effect (**v 15**) that "those who live" as a result of that death "might no longer live for themselves but for him who for their sake died and was raised". Even though it is crystal clear that what Paul is driving at is the necessity of Christ-like love in ministry, *how he gets there* isn't quite so obvious, and these statements about Christ's death have caused no end of controversy.

So when he says, "Christ died for all"—does he mean everyone without exception? Was Paul a **universalist**? Or, given the fact that in verse 15, he is clearly talking about believers, did Christ die for everyone but was he only raised for believers? These are tricky questions that have divided people over the years, but I think that the most natural way to read these verses is as referring to the same group of people all the way through—namely, Christian believers, for whom Christ died and rose again. His point then is that having been united with Christ by faith in his death and resurrection, we have already died to ourselves, and the only real option for us is to live for Christ, which, as Paul goes on to explain, means loving other people.

If we take this on board, we will refuse to look at anyone—especially, I think, brothers and sisters in Christ—"according to the flesh" (**v 16**). Paul adds that we, meaning him in particular, got it so spectacularly wrong about Jesus that it should cure us of making damning judgments about anyone else.

It also means, in the words of **verse 17**, that "if anyone is in Christ, he is a new creation. The old has passed away; behold, the new has come." There isn't actually a verb in verse 17—which makes it hard to tie down exactly what Paul is saying. "If anyone is in Christ, new creation" is how it reads in the original. Paul may be saying, as the ESV translates it, that anyone who is in Christ is a new creation—or, more likely, that for anyone who is in Christ, the **new creation** has already broken in, transforming the way in which we look at everyone and everything. Either way, Paul's point is very clear—the love that God has shown us in Christ's death and resurrection drives us to love people as the Lord Jesus Christ did.

So do we love people as Christ loved people—by giving himself to die for them? Do we want to? Do we aim for this? Is it even on our radar? Reading both 1 and 2 Corinthians suggests that the church at Corinth did need some persuasion to make love a priority. And I suspect we are the same. Bible Christians can prioritise truth over love. But loving as Christ did is at the core of authentic Christian ministry—whether because we know we are new creations, or because our perspective has been completely revolutionised by knowing that the new creation has come. The truth is that if our grasp of the gospel increases, then so will our love for other people. This is the measure, the gauge, of the length and breadth and depth of the work of Christ in us. Didn't Jesus say repeatedly that

> If our grasp of the gospel increases, then so will our love for other people.

"by this all people will know that you are my disciples, if you have love for one another" (John 13:34-35)?

We pursue gospel relationships relentlessly

One of the remarkable things about Paul is that despite the number of churches with which he has links and the number of people he knows, he still sticks with the Corinthians come what may. What is it that drives him in this? It's Paul's doctrine of reconciliation, which is where chapter 5 ends.

There is remarkably little space in the New Testament devoted to reconciliation as an explicit topic—reconciliation language occurs only in Paul's writings, and even then only three times: in 1 Corinthians 7, in Romans 5, and here in 2 Corinthians 5. At one level, it is a relatively uncommon doctrine which is barely mentioned. Yet at another, it takes us right to the heart of the gospel, and is the heartbeat of the New Testament, because the work of reconciliation takes us to the very core of the work of the Christ our mediator.

In the succinct statement on **5:18-19**, Paul sums up all that God has done for us in Christ *and* what he call *us* to do like this. God has "reconciled us to himself in Christ", doing everything that was needed to restore our relationship with him. Just as God had intervened in Paul's life on the Damascus road to disarm an enemy and make him a friend, so he works in all of us through the gospel. In particular, God has set up a way for our sin to be *counted against* Jesus, who paid the penalty for our sin and faced the wrath that it rightly provoked by dying in our place. This message—the message of reconciliation—is the one which we have now been entrusted with. This is the message which we proclaim to our world.

> The message of reconciliation is the one which we have now been entrusted with. This is the message we proclaim to our world.

We then come to **verse 20**, which stands at the heart of this entire section, and perhaps the entire letter of 2 Corinthians: "Therefore, we are ambassadors for Christ, God making his appeal through us". An ambassador (*presbeuomen*) was normally sent as a representative of a lesser nation to curry favour with a local superpower like Rome. But God has **condescended** in the gospel to send people like us, making not his demands but his *appeal through us.* This is God's method. This is the task with which we have been charged. J.I. Packer writes:

> "His royal master had given him a message to proclaim; his whole business therefore was to deliver that message with exact and studious faithfulness, adding nothing, altering nothing, and omitting nothing. And he was to deliver it not as another man's bright ideas, needing to be beautified with the cosmetics and high heels of fashionable learning in order to make people look at it, but as the word of God, spoken in Christ's name, carrying Christ's authority, and to be authenticated in the hearers by the convincing power of Christ's Spirit."
>
> (*Evangelism and the Sovereignty of God,* p 43-44)

But notice where Paul goes with this: "We implore you on behalf of Christ, be reconciled to God". Paul's great concern in all this is that his relationship with the Corinthians is out of step with the gospel. So he calls not pagans but his Christian brothers and sisters in Corinth to be reconciled to God—now that comes as a bit of a shock. Think about the implications of this: if our relationships with one another, our gospel partnerships, are disrupted, then we can't simply let it go—we can't retreat and sing happily "You in your small corner, and I in mine". That simply isn't an option. Because God has reconciled us to himself through the gospel, then we must pursue authentic gospel relationships. This is how God's reconciling power is proclaimed and demonstrated to the world. This is the message we need to speak and live out.

James Denney, a Scottish theologian of the early 20th century, wrote this:

"A reconciled man, preaching Christ as the way of recon-ciliation and preaching him in the temper and spirit which the experience of reconciliation creates, is the most effec-tive mediator of Christ's reconciling power"

(*The Christian Doctrine of Reconciliation*, p 8)

Because of Jesus' work of reconciliation—his sin-bearing, righteous-ness-giving, relationship-restoring work on the cross and in his resur-rection—we are people who relentlessly pursue gospel relationships: who are prepared to face pain, and say hard things, and take the initiative over and over again to pursue things until they are right, because this is the way of the gospel.

Reconciliation is the way in which God has dealt with his wrath and our sin in Christ. To restore our relationship to that of delight and intimacy with God as we revel in his glory, demands a massive reversal, which happened when God himself took the initiative to heal this rift, dealing with his own wrath and our guilt at the same time. How did he do that? He did it by making "him to be sin who knew no sin, so that in him we might become the righteousness of God" (**v 21**). There is so much packed into this relatively simple phrase. Paul, it seems, is drawing on Isaiah 53 to describe Jesus Christ, God's perfect, flaw-less Son, who became our sin-bearer, standing in as our substitute, to bring about a radical change in us. We who were guilty are now joined to Christ, sharing in his righteousness and enjoying the peace which flows to us in a restored relationship with the Father. No wonder Calvin called this the *wonderful exchange.* It is a swap unlike any other because it actually brings about transformation.

We could spend pages unpacking just this single, astounding phrase. But for our purposes, the main thing is that we see where Paul goes with this. Paul writes this because of his longing *to see his relationship with the Corinthians restored.*

Recalibrating our lives

This is a hard chapter. That's partly because of Paul's slightly frustrating habit of introducing massive theological concepts in throwaway lines to support his relatively simple appeals to the Corinthians. But mostly it's because what he says is mind-blowing. So let's not miss the massive implications of his deeply vulnerable attempts to get the Corinthians to stand with him: as men and women in Christ we look to the future; we fear God, not people; we love people as Christ did, and we pursue real gospel relationships. Which prompts a very obvious question: *do we?*

> Recalibrate your priorities, so that you really are only concerned about pleasing God, rather than people.

So do we look to the future? Fear God, not people? Love people as Christ did? Do we pursue gospel relationships relentlessly? It doesn't come naturally, but this is the real thing. It may be that you need to repent of your focus on the immediate and ask God to lift your head so that you might look forward to what's ahead for all those in Christ, and those without him. Or it may be that you need to recalibrate your priorities, so that you really are only concerned about pleasing God, rather than people. Or it could be that you have to face the fact that you don't honestly love anyone, other than yourself. Perhaps the idea of loving another selflessly is a real struggle for you, and you need to throw yourself on Christ for help. Or, conceivably, you have quietly given up on relationships with Christian brothers and sisters, or you may have given yourself licence to harden your hearts against someone, and you need to revive your efforts to be reconciled to them in the gospel. For this is what God asks of us in this passage.

The message of the gospel is both deeply theological and profoundly relational. It is both truth and love. It is both believing and living. It is in our heads and in our hearts and lives. May God work this message so thoroughly into our consciousness that we can say with Richard Hooker, the English Puritan:

"Let it be counted folly or frenzy or whatsoever. It is our wisdom and our comfort; we care for no knowledge in the world but this, that man has sinned and God has suffered; that God has made himself the sin of men and that men are made the righteousness of God."

(Sermon on Habakkuk 1:4, 1585)

Questions for reflection

1. To what extent are you a people-pleaser? How should the gospel reshape that instinct?

2. If we look at other people through the lens of the gospel, what difference will it make?

3. Who do you need to start (or restart) loving with Christ's love as you pursue reconciliation?

6. MAKE-YOUR-MIND-UP TIME

Imagine for a moment that you are a teenage girl. You hear your parents call from the kitchen, "Dinner's ready" Do you…

a. completely ignore them;?

b. say, "I'm coming" and completely ignore them?

c. say "I'll be there when I have finished this question?

d. act as if you are coming immediately, but then disappear into the bathroom? Or…

e. move promptly and without fuss to the table, pausing only to offer to help on the way?

Of course the problem with (a) is that it does tend to raise the temperature of the family atmosphere. Come to think of it, answers (b) to (d) have the same effect. So much so that any response other than (e) will quickly lead to a further multiple-choice question: *are you going to…*

a. get to the table before I can count to 5? Or…

b. suffer a punishment more terrible than any human being can bear—lose your phone for a week?

So far in his letters to the church in Corinth, Paul has wooed and persuaded and cajoled and appealed and commanded. The Corinthians have defied, prevaricated, dragged their heels and come up with all kinds of excuses. They have pushed Paul to the point where he lays it on the line with them. They have two choices: either they need to side with him and the gospel or face the reality that they have departed from the gospel of the Lord Jesus Christ.

All the way back in 2 Corinthians 2, Paul began to describe the shape of the authentic Christian life (which is also the shape of his gospel-driven ministry) in an attempt to woo the Corinthians back to him and to the gospel. Now, finally, in chapter 6, his argument reaches its climax in a passage which is carefully argued, incredibly blunt and deeply challenging in equal measure. We'll unpack Paul's extended appeal to this church he had planted to stick with him and Christ in five simple imperatives.

1. Act now!

Paul's opening salvo in this section packs a real punch, as he insists that he is *working together with God*, which invests his words with real authority, as he *urges* them *not to receive the grace of God in vain* (**6:1**).

Appealing to people, urging people, even commanding people to respond appropriately to the gospel are vital in gospel ministry. Calvin, commenting on this verse, said, "It is not enough to teach if you do not also urge". As Paul has already said in this letter, "God makes his appeal through us" (5:20), which means we need to learn to speak the gospel ourselves with a quiet, gentle, substantial authority that comes not from us, but from the words of God himself in the gospel. I suspect that for many of us, and perhaps particularly for you if you are under 35, this will prove to be quite a challenge. The relational sensitivity and strong empathy of today's world is great—but we must still learn to urge and even command one another in the love of the Lord Jesus. And we all must take seriously the possibility of "receiving the grace of God in vain".

There's a lot in this chapter for us to learn *from Paul himself*, as he models how to inspire people to radical commitment to Christ by living a gospel-shaped life. But there are also several places, as we'll see, where what he actually writes *to* the Corinthians cuts right through our defences and forces us to face some very searching realities about ourselves—and here's the first: it's possible to *receive the grace of God in vain*.

> Paul's fear was that their faith would come to nothing: that they would "receive the grace of God in vain".

The Corinthians had known Paul for years. He had lived in Corinth, teaching them week by week. After Paul left, he kept up a running correspondence with them, writing them the longest letter in the New Testament, and now this letter (which is not short). They had privileged access to a man who was surely the greatest theologian-teacher there has ever been. Yet Paul's fear was that it would come to nothing: that they would "receive the grace of God in vain".

Many of us reading this book will be part of churches where the Bible is taught carefully, faithfully and systematically. Many of us have been taught and trained and nurtured by all kinds of people. We might also have received an education which means that reading an entire book about one part of the Bible isn't daunting. We have the financial resources to spend money on books, and the God-given good sense to buy books on the Bible. But the problem is that it is still possible for us to have all this and it make no real and lasting difference—to "receive the grace of God in vain", and end up nowhere, with the gospel having made no lasting difference in our lives. It's a chilling prospect. The picture is of an empty house, or an empty jug, or empty hands. And the warning encompasses past, present and future. We may have done this in the past, be doing it now or may do it in the future. It's possible to receive the grace of God in vain at any point. So how do we avoid this? What's the alternative? It's actually quite simple, and it's spelled out in **6:2**.

Paul quotes Isaiah 49:8 and makes both a simple point and a more complex one. The simple point flows out of the fact that to introduce the quotation, he notes that *God says*... God speaks in the present tense. It would very easy to allow our eye to run past that and miss its significance: God is speaking—his word is still "live". What God said back then, he is still saying today. But Paul is also making a point which is a little more tricky to pick up.

In Isaiah 49, God is speaking to his servant, whom we now know to be Jesus: "In a favourable time I listened to you, and in a day of salvation I have helped you". Isaiah is saying that God has listened to his servant, come to his aid and helped the servant to fulfil his rescue mission. Which is exactly what happened as Jesus came and set up a new covenant, drawing people like you and me into it. The *day of salvation* was the day of the servant, the day of Jesus. And now? Now, Paul says, the day of salvation continues through the servants of the servant! "Behold, now is the favourable time; behold, now is the day of salvation." Paul insists that *his* ministry is an extension of *Jesus'* ministry, and as he preaches the same gospel, the Corinthians really need to listen and respond. He says that *right now* is, literally, the most acceptable time there is for embracing the gospel. And if that was true as Paul wrote to the Corinthians, then it is also true today as we open up the Bible, and it's true every time this gospel is proclaimed. Which means it falls on us right now to listen and respond, lest we receive the grace of God in vain.

Paul's point then is this: if we are to avoid receiving the grace of God in vain, then we need to take this very, very seriously. The way of discipleship is the way of listening to God speak in the here and now, every day, and responding on the spot. The alternative is to slip into a dangerously Corinthian mentality, where we say (usually silently), "I know you are speaking to me Lord—I have taken a note of it and will respond in due course". But when God addresses us, it has to take priority over everything. So is there anything you know God has been addressing in your life but you have been trying to file it away for consideration in due course? If there is, then now would be a great time to deal with it, lest you receive the grace of God in vain.

2. Embrace reality!

There are several places where Paul gives us a snapshot of life as apostle to the **Gentiles**, and it isn't entirely what we might have expected! But before we dive into the beatings and slander, we need to make sure we've understood *why* Paul takes the Corinthians—and us—through all this. *He desperately wants the Corinthians to get the fact that this is what real ministry looks like.* In their success-mad, reputation-driven, ultra-ambitious hearts and culture, Paul longs for them to realise that looking slick means nothing, that having a great Wikipedia entry isn't worth the papyrus it's written on, and that sounding impressive without substance will get you nowhere. He longs for them to accept and embrace the reality of authentic gospel ministry. So he gathers up all that he has said so far about the real deal—about authentic gospel ministry—in 2 Corinthians 6:3-10.

All that he writes is governed by the principle that "as servants of God we commend ourselves in every way" (**v 4**), which, for Paul, means going to great lengths to make sure that no unnecessary difficulties are caused *for other people* (**v 3**). This is what makes gospel ministry so demanding—this is why Paul was willing to put up with all this and more. It's because if we have been mastered by the gospel, then it isn't actually about us any more but about other people. And if it's about other people, then we will do everything in our power to deal with anything about ourselves—what we say and how we live—that has any possibility of obscuring the gospel.

> If we have been mastered by the gospel, then life isn't actually about us any more but about other people.

This desire to present Christ to people will make us willing to stay up late and get up early, to take low blows and late hits; it will shape what we watch and eat and drive and wear. It is this authenticity, this relentless drive to ensure that the gospel is on full view and illustrated by every part of our lives, that Paul models and calls us to, following him as we follow Christ. This is gospel-shaped ministry. And Paul says, *Come on—you know that this is the real thing—embrace it*!

There is some discussion about whether "by great endurance" in verse 4 is the headline for Paul's list or the first item in it, but either way, it's clear that Paul starts off with a list of struggles—all in the plural, introduced by the Greek preposition "in". "In afflictions, hardships, calamities, beatings, imprisonments, riots, labours, sleepless nights, hunger". He then switches in **verses 6-7** to a list of eight resources or graces—all in the singular, still introduced by "in": "... purity, knowledge, patience, kindness, the Holy Spirit, genuine love; by truthful speech, and by the power of God; with the weapons of righteousness for the right hand and for the left". He then moves on to the ups and downs of this ministry (introduced by "through") in **verse 8**: "...through honour and dishonour, through slander and praise". Finally he lays out the ways in which God reverses the disadvantages that Paul faces for the good of the gospel. Even though Paul and his companions are treated as fakes, nobodies, weaklings, criminals, killjoys and scroungers, they have all that they need and more in Christ.

It's some list. Here is faithfulness. Here is authenticity. Here is integrity. Here is what God is calling us to. So have you embraced this? We could spend ages working through this list, highlighting the nuance of every term that Paul uses, but I think it's more useful to ask four questions which flow out of the four movements of the list.

1. *Are you ready for the rest of your life to be hard?* It really will be. The particular shape of difficulty we may face is unpredictable—but the fact that life will be hard is not. Let me break it to you gently—you will not be well paid. You will not be a much sought-after dinner guest. You will be excluded, sidelined and whispered about. You may be sued. It is going to be hard.

2. *Are you committed to using only gospel-shaped means and methods in ministry?* No doubt some of those philosopher-types who

had so damaged the work in Corinth were terribly impressive. The fact that they were, in all likelihood, **Sophists**, who were the origin of sophistication, is a clue to that. But Paul had a markedly different approach. His priorities, in verse 6, were "purity" (a rare word, which probably means something like straightforwardness, sincerity or guilelessness), "knowledge" (referring here to the knowledge of God through Christ) "patience" and "kindness". These were very different from the kind of entitled behaviour so typical of those making a living on the philosophy circuit. They emphasise the fact that he could achieve nothing without "the Holy Spirit". Paul also prioritises the "genuine love" for the people he is speaking to, as he brings them "the word of truth" (a better translation than the ESV's "by truthful speech"), and the power of God "with the weapons of righteousness for the right hand and for the left". That may be a reference to Ephesians 6, or, more likely, an expression of dependence on God working through his word.

Basically, this is Paul's philosophy of ministry—and practically speaking, I'm not sure there is a more important concept for anyone who is committed to serving Jesus wholeheartedly in the long-term. What are the non-negotiables? What are the key things that are locked into your mind and practice because you have been convinced through God's word that this is his way? For Paul, his philosophy of ministry drips out of this passage and countless others. He proclaims Christ from God's word in the power of the Spirit, backed up by his own authenticity—love for people, patience with them and refusing to promote himself, look down on others or use manipulation. Have you got this kind of gospel-shaped philosophy of ministry locked into your brain, so that, whatever part you play in the body of Christ, it will show these same characteristics? Which takes us to a third question...

3. *Are you prepared for the fact that you will be praised and damned in equal measure?* As I was writing this, I started to type, "Having had plenty of both, I can honestly say that for me, praise is

much harder to cope with." Then I thought for a moment, and changed it to "being slandered is harder…" but you know what? Both possibilities mentioned in 2 Corinthians 6:8 are really tough to take. To be in ministry is to be confronted with the temptation of growing big-headed on the one hand and being crushed by shame and despair on the other. They are actually equal and opposite forms of the same thing—one is pride on a good day, the other pride on a bad one. Both boasting and self-pity have the same root—acting as if the way we feel about ourselves is what matters! And how do we extricate ourselves from this trap? That takes us to the final question.

4. *Are you convinced that you can only find security and satisfaction in Christ?* In the series of "matching pairs" with which Paul brings this section to a close in **verses 9-10**, the crucial thing is what turns the negative into the positive. What makes the difference? It's the security that we have in the Lord Jesus Christ. Paul knows he is not an imposter but one who speaks the truth in Christ, who is known by Christ, who has tasted new life in Christ, and whose destiny is untouchable because he is safe in Christ. All of us with Paul can rejoice in Christ, can hold out life to others in Christ, can have all things in Christ. It is *in Christ* that we have the resources, the strength and the energy we need to serve him.

Questions for reflection

1. Paul is very clear on the need to listen to God and do what he says *right now*, lest we "receive the grace of God in vain". What might receiving the grace of God in vain look like for you?

2. Why does getting the gospel across to people with clarity matter so much?

3. What does God promise us as those who are in Christ? What can we expect life to be like?

PART TWO

Paul's last-ditch attempt to persuade the Corinthians to stick with him and the gospel began with an appeal to act now and to face the reality of belonging to Christ. In the second half of this chapter, he piles on three more commands:

3. Open your hearts!

Paul assures them that his heart is wide open (**6:11**), that the relational issues can easily be resolved by the Corinthians (**v 12**) and tells them to widen their hearts also (**v 13**). The relational issue between the apostle and the church plant is not Paul's overbearing or domineering attitude—it is whether the Corinthians are willing to open their hearts to Paul.

One of the trickiest issues for anyone who wants to be involved in gospel ministry of any kind is working out who to work closely with. How do we work out whether to throw ourselves into gospel partnership with someone or steer well clear of them? Which is more important? Close alignment in theology and philosophy of ministry or the command to love one another? I think most of us, if we're honest, tend instinctively to veer to one of those two poles. Some of us are naturally cynical and suspicious, and some of us are more naturally gullible. For some of us, relating to others is reduced to a matter of pure truth. For others, truth goes out the window, and it's all about love. So how do we negotiate this relational minefield? We copy Paul by being full on with both ways of relating. We speak freely and are completely upfront and unapologetic about the truth, but also we unreservedly open our hearts to anyone who is willing to stand with us.

4. Stick with us!

For the record, I think it is a terrible idea for Christians to marry non-Christians, and the Bible makes that very clear in many places. I also think that smoking and excessive use of alcohol are bad for you and should generally be avoided by all sensible people everywhere. However, I am also convinced that being unequally yoked is not primarily about marriage, and that Paul introduces the fact that we are the "temple of the Lord" to do something more than persuading us all to switch to cholesterol-lowering spread and to cut back our consumption of regular Coke. In fact, these verses are, in many ways, the climax of the argument that Paul has been developing since chapter 2, as he calls the Corinthians to stick with him.

Look at what Paul *actually* says in **6:14**:

> "Do not be unequally yoked with unbelievers. For what partnership has righteousness with lawlessness? Or what fellowship has light with darkness?"

In the first place, Paul is calling the Corinthians to stick with him—and by extension to stick with Christ and the gospel, rather than opting to run with those who are offering an alternative view of the world. He isn't offering a template for how we relate to people who aren't Christians in general. This isn't about entering business partnership, or only using Christian electricians. This is about sticking with the gospel, which becomes even clearer in **verse 15**. Paul is characterising his opponents (for the very first time) as unbelievers. Their teaching, their theology and their philosophy of ministry are so far from that of Christ that he is left with no option but to "out them" as *unbelievers*. This isn't about personality or popularity; for Paul, this goes right to the heart of the gospel.

> Paul is calling them to stick with Christ and the gospel, rather run with those who are offering an alternative view of the world.

Throughout the whole letter up to this point, Paul has been sketching the profile of gospel-shaped integrity and authenticity—he has been describing the real thing. Now he spells out the implications of this. It means that those who oppose him are actually on the side of Satan. "Belial" is an Old Testament term derived from the words for "worthless". The name was connected to idols in the Old Testament and became connected with Satan in later Christian theology. Paul develops this line of reasoning in **verse 16,** "What agreement has the temple of God with idols? For we are the temple of the living God." We, the church, are the new-covenant temple—it is in us and among us that God has taken up residence by his Spirit. It is here, in the church, that God has set up his outposts of the kingdom so that it will grow and spread in anticipation of the return of Christ. *How could we possibly invite those who are actively opposing Christ to set up shop in his church?* Paul has just urged the Corinthians to be open to him and to the gospel; now he calls on them to shut down some options—and, in particular, to slam the gate shut in the face of these pseudo-Christian philosophers.

Paul backs up these tough conclusions with a string of Old Testament quotations. First, he quotes a series of promises from Leviticus 26:11-12 and Ezekiel 37:27: "As God said, 'I will make my dwelling among them and walk among them, and I will be their God, and they shall be my people.'". From the beginning, God had committed himself to making it possible for people like us to live with a God like him. To side with these misguided philosophers—to walk away from the gospel—was, in effect, to reject God, which is why Paul continues, now quoting from Isaiah 52:11: "Therefore go out from their midst, and be separate from them, says the Lord, and touch no unclean thing", and then Ezekiel 20:41, "then I will welcome you", followed by 2 Samuel 7:14: "and I will be a father to you, and you shall be sons and daughters to me [possibly influenced by Isaiah 43:6] says the Lord Almighty."

The striking thing about all these quotations is that they are all drawn from contexts dealing with God's intimate relationship with his people, which was expressed and embodied by his presence in the temple. God poured out his grace on his people, calling them to obedience so that they could enjoy life in his presence, symbolised by the temple itself. Now that Christ has come, through our union with him, we are the temple—we are the place where God himself is and where he can be known and enjoyed by people saved by grace for obedience. This is new-covenant, gospel-shaped life. Paul insists that to reject him is to reject the gospel, which is to reject Christ and to undercut all that is described here.

It is intriguing that Paul quotes 2 Samuel 7:14, one of the key texts in the Old Testament that points to Jesus, the messiah, and *applies it to us.* In Christ, we share in the sonship of the Messiah, and, contrary to the caricature of grumpy old misogynist Paul, women get to join in too! But make sure you get his point: how could we trade in any or all of this for the sake of some second-rate fusion of Sophist philosophy and Corinthian culture?

At one level, 2 Corinthians **6:14-18** may not seem to be the most readily applicable part of this letter to us—but let's make no mistake: to seek to live for Christ is to expose ourselves to an atmosphere which will constantly encourage us to swap the gospel for something that promises more but ultimately delivers nothing. This has been the weakness of the human race from Genesis 3—over and over again we repeat the mistake of our first parents and give away everything for nothing. And it may be that even today, what we need more than anything is to take hold of the fact that God offers us himself in the gospel, and to walk away from every alternative as nothing more than a dumb idol. And you may not feel the pull of those idols today, but one day, you will, and for Paul, forewarned is very definitely forearmed.

So, Paul is saying, act now, embrace reality, open your hearts, stick with us, and summing it all up…

5. Commit!

What are we to do with all this? These extravagant Old Testament gospel promises which Paul has just included—that God will come and make his home with us, that he will be our God and to make us his

people—should move us and moti-
vate us to walk away from spiritual
adultery, and commit ourselves to a
gospel-shaped,   gospel-empowered
faithfulness. That's what Paul is talking about when he makes this remarkable statement: "Let us cleanse
ourselves from every defilement of
body and spirit, bringing holiness
to completion in the fear of God"
(2 Corinthians **7:1**).

> Over and over
> again we repeat
> the mistake of
> our first parents
> and give away
> everything for
> nothing.

That last phrase—"bringing holiness to completion in the fear of
God"—is strangely overlooked by most commentators, but it is vital to
the conclusion of Paul's argument.

Reflecting on what God has done for us in the Lord Jesus Christ
should ultimately lead us to throw ourselves into living for him in a
way which reflects that we belong to the one and only God. That is,
we should live holy lives. And we should do this for the rest of our
lives, until God has finished the process of making us more like the
Lord Jesus. And we should do it in the awareness that we are living
with and before and for the God of all power and holiness, to whom
we will all give an account for the way in which we lived. Back in 5:11,
Paul said that this fear of the Lord is the reason why he seeks to proclaim Christ ("Therefore, knowing the fear of the Lord, we persuade
others"). Now he extends this to explain that the fear of the Lord is
the reason he lives for Christ, and the reason why the Corinthians
should commit to him, to the gospel and to Christ himself.

Isn't it sobering that the "fear of the Lord" is what motivates
Paul? Of course, he is moved and shaped by the gospel of grace. But
the fact remains that the God who reaches down to us in the Lord
Jesus Christ is the God of the universe, the Maker and Judge of all
things, the one before whom everyone will one day bow. This is why
Paul calls the Philippians to work out their salvation "with fear and

trembling" (Philippians 2:12), and the Colossian slaves to "obey in everything those who are your earthly masters, not by way of **eye-service**, as people-pleasers, but with sincerity of heart, fearing the Lord" (Colossians 3:22). This is why he tells the Corinthians to "bring holiness to completion in the fear of God". This is not a game. God himself is speaking to us in the Lord Jesus Christ, the One who died and rose again for us. This is the word of God to us today in the light of all that he has done and is doing and will do for us in the Lord Jesus: "Bring holiness to completion in the fear of God".

Let's commit ourselves to him afresh in repentance and faith.

Questions for reflection

1. For many of us, either because of our personality or experience, it's hard to open our hearts to others. Why is that, and what can we do about it?

2. How should we relate to other Christians?

3. Paul tells the Corinthians to "bring holiness to completion in the fear of God". What do you think that looks like in practice?

7. BECAUSE I'M HAPPY

Clap along if you feel like a room without a roof

I have never been entirely persuaded by the philosophical undergirdings of Pharrell Williams' hit song—I have never felt like a room without a roof. But you can't deny that he *is* happy—or at least he *was* while he was singing it. But the really remarkable thing is that when we come to 2 Corinthians 7, despite everything he is experiencing, the apostle Paul does actually sound happy!

Chapters 1 – 6 are just about the most raw, full-on, up-close-and-personal, deeply intense chapters of the whole New Testament. Paul has been fighting desperately to win the hearts and minds of the church family in Corinth, and we have got the strong sense that for most of the letter so far, he hasn't had any real confidence that it was going to come off. The future of the church he has planted seems to be up in the air. He is laying everything on the line to help them stay on track, and then suddenly, just like that, the mood changes, and the apostle is apparently dancing for joy! *What's going on?*

The explanation is quite straightforward. Life is complex. Even when we are facing big issues, they are never the whole story. Sometimes we are facing a huge problem, but once we've dealt with that, the underlying situation is really quite encouraging. And that's exactly what's happening here. For the first six chapters, Paul has been speaking to those who are wavering—the people who have been influenced by their city and their favourite philosophers, and aren't too sure about Paul—but now we get the rest of the picture. Paul is *happy.* And as he rejoices, the apostle maps out what it takes for all of us to *be happy servants of the Lord Jesus*!

2 Corinthians 7 is one of those sections of Paul's letter where it isn't so much the recipients who fill the viewfinder as the apostle Paul himself. By the way in which he deals with and responds to and encourages the Corinthians, Paul doesn't really tell us much about them. But in the kindness of God, Paul shows us how he operates, and he manages to provide us with a marvellous template for a lifetime of happy gospel ministry. Of course, what we learn about the importance of happiness in gospel ministry in 2 Corinthians 7 does come in a context where Paul has said rather a lot about the unavoidable reality of suffering for the gospel. We have seen plenty of that so far. But, for Paul, there is always real joy in ministry even as we suffer, and that's why he gives us four steps to genuine Christian joy.

Step 1: Pursue integrity

As Paul again appeals to the Corinthians to "make room in your hearts for us" (**v 2**), he backs that up with a straightforward defence of his integrity. He says, "We [that is, the apostle and his co-workers] have wronged no one, we have corrupted no one, we have taken advantage of no one". Calvin says that Paul is highlighting the three dangers that anyone in gospel ministry faces: (i) being too harsh, (ii) leading people astray through teaching wrong ideas and (iii) being greedy. (See John Calvin, *The Second Letter of Paul to the Corinthians*, p 95). Paul had done everything in his power to make sure that he didn't slip into any of those things—*he pursued integrity*. This is the first step to joy.

Paul has already spoken in this letter about the importance of a clear conscience (see 1:12). He knows that if he is going to be able to sleep at night, if he is to avoid beating himself up endlessly, if he is to find joy in his ministry—a key step is to make sure that his ministry has godly consistency, that it has integrity. Not that it is perfect—for no ministry can ever be that—but there are no glaring contradictions in the way in which he speaks and leads and teaches, no gaping holes in what he has and hasn't done. So, it seems, he regularly examines himself to check on his tone, his content and his motives.

> Paul regularly examines himself to check on his tone, his content and his motives.

So here is a simple template for you in the years to come: when you are working alongside others in God's family, ask yourself regularly, "Am I being too harsh?" There are times when you will be. It's hard when we throw ourselves into ministry—and specific projects in particular—not to get a bit cranky when it isn't going well, or when people say they'll come and don't, or they just never show up at all. It's easy to slip into thinking that if it weren't for *these people*, things would be going really well. But it's really important that we don't let bitterness or resentment or even anger eat us up. We need to be able to say, with Paul, "We have wronged no one".

We also need to be able to hold our heads up and say, "I haven't misled anyone". The truth matters. It really matters. And that means we need to be prepared to work really hard for our whole lives to ensure that what we believe and are passing on to others doesn't veer off course over time. So ask yourself: *am I doing everything in my power to teach the gospel in all its richness?*

Unfortunately, this is much harder than it looks! It's easy to ride our own particular hobby horses more than is healthy. It's easy to gradually and unwittingly start to leave out key aspects of the gospel. That's why it's so important for people who are going to be teachers in the church to invest in the best possible training they can get, soaking up as much of the gospel as they can—because that gives them the best possible start. That's why systematic **expository** preaching, week by week, book by book, is far and away the best diet for the church, because it allows the word of God itself to set the agenda, forcing us to deal with subjects that we wouldn't naturally touch with a barge pole, making us think and rethink as we're confronted with new issues, or old issues we didn't quite get the last time. And that's also why it's so very important to keep learning, and make sure that we are still being taught the Bible by other people (both living and dead), because this is how our own teaching will be corrected and pulled back into shape.

And we need to ask ourselves: *have I slipped into thinking that I want more?*

Paul does seem to have been very sensitive to any accusation that he was in ministry for what he could get. While insisting that pastors should be paid, he refused to take a salary, becoming the original tent-making tent-maker. And when dealing with believers in Corinth, one of *the* most lucrative dates on the philosophy circuit, he made sure that they knew that he and his companions were not, "like so many, peddlers of God's word, but ... men of sincerity, as commissioned by God, in the sight of God ... speak in Christ" (2:17). Paul made sure that no one could say that he was in it for the money. And that's a great way to be...

> Do everything to make sure that money is never an issue in your life.

So do everything to make sure that money is never an issue in your life. Whether you are a pastor or a church member, don't take a job just because it is well-paid or turn one down because it isn't. Don't whine about what you do or don't get. Don't look for privileges, and resist any attempt by others to put you on a pedestal or your name on a plaque. Of course, we have a responsibility to look after our families, and we need to eat, and I'm not saying that there isn't hard thinking to be done and even hard conversations to have about financial realities, but do everything in your power to keep money in its place, as you fight against greed.

Of course, the reason why Paul was so passionate about all this—the reason why Paul pursued integrity with such single-mindedness—was Christ himself. Christ had met Paul on the road to Damascus and turned his life around. Christ had brought him to life. Christ had given him a new purpose—to call Gentiles to the obedience which flows from faith. Christ had changed and equipped him through the Spirit, and, because of that, Paul was willing to do anything to get this message across—and that meant laying a foundation of integrity as he sought to preach Christ. Paul knew that whatever missteps he may have taken along the way, his ministry had real integrity. And in the context of 2 Corinthians 7, it is *this integrity* which is the first step to being a happy gospel worker—because on the one hand, it means we can sleep at night knowing that we have given our best to Christ, and on the other, it frees us up to take step 2.

Step 2: Invest in people

The most striking thing about this chapter is the depth of emotional engagement which Paul's words convey. He appeals to the Corinthians to "make room in their hearts" for him in verse 2. But this isn't mere rhetoric. Look at how he speaks of the Corinthians in **verses 3-4**: he says, "You are in our hearts, to die together and to live together ... I have great pride in you ... In all our affliction, I am overflowing with joy." This is the church which gave Paul the most intense, longest-lasting headaches—and yet how he speaks about them! He *loves* these people deeply. He has poured himself out for their wellbeing. And it isn't just them. He speaks about Titus with the same passion in verses 5-7.

Macedonia was one of Paul's favourite destinations, but not this time. He was stressed about the Corinthians and stressed about Titus, who hadn't shown up (**v 5**)—and remember, in the first century there was no alternative but to wait around and hope. When Titus did at last arrive, Paul's relief was palpable; he records that "God, who comforts the downcast, comforted us by the coming of Titus" (**v 6**). But not only was he comforted by Titus' presence; he was also relieved to get his news from Corinth. Paul writes that he was *delighted* when he heard "of your longing, your mourning, your zeal for me" (**v 7**). This really is a win-win situation for Paul. Titus shows up, and that thrills him, and Titus gives the news that the Corinthians, rather than having rejected him, care deeply about him.

As if all that weren't enough, Paul took real joy in Titus' delight in the Corinthians (**v 13**). Do you hear how invested Paul is in both Titus and the Corinthians? Paul, it seems, had also been talking Titus up to the Corinthians (**v 14**)—which, in a fallen world, is always a bit risky. I remember boasting once about how friendly our much-loved (and genuinely loving) church family in Dublin was. That was fine until another minister came to visit and not a single person spoke to him or his wife, which he was quick to tell me in an email on Monday morning. But Titus came through for Paul with flying colours: "For whatever boasts I made to him about you, I was not put to shame" (v 14). It turns out that Paul hadn't just boasted about Titus to the Corinthians; he had boasted about the church of Corinth to Titus—and it all came off, much to Paul's relief. As a result of all this, Titus (**v 15**) and Paul (**v 16**) were both very happy gospel workers.

Paul's joy is directly related to his *investment in people* (see also, for example, 1 Thessalonians 2:5-8). Of course, investing in people means opening ourselves up to a lifetime of concern—to sleepless nights, and painful conversations, and anxious waits. As Calvin says, "Christ's servants hardly ever have respite from fears". But *investing in people* is also the second step to real joy in ministry. In fact, for Paul, ministry *is* investing in people.

So what does investing in people actually look like? How do we do it?

- *Investing in people flows out of love for people.* This is where we need to begin. Ministry that isn't born of love for people will be miserable for you and miserable for the people you are supposedly serving! There is nothing sadder—or, I suspect, more damaging—than loveless ministry, where there is no real investment in people. Real investment flows from love. And this love takes time to grow; but if we don't love people, then we won't invest properly in them, and there will be a joy deficit all round. So we need to start by asking God to help us to love the people we know.

- *Investing in people is costly and time-consuming.* The hardest thing about ministry is *always* people. It doesn't matter how extrovert or introvert you may be, it doesn't matter how much you like the person or you struggle with them. Investing in people always drains energy and sucks up time. But remember—people don't take you away from your ministry; *they are your ministry.*

- *Investing in people includes training but is much more than training.* Investing in people means both handing on a set of skills and sharing life with them. It means loving them through their foolishness and stubbornness and pain and sadness, as well as walking with them when things are going well. Investing lov-

> Investing lovingly in people is messy and unpredictable and costly.

ingly in people is messy and unpredictable and costly. It means hanging in with the people we love for the long haul. It means being willing to stick with them when being with them is a burden to us and a drain on our energy.

- *Investing in people brings us into step with God himself.* Jonathan Edwards, in his epic book *A Dissertation Concerning the End for Which God Created the World,* makes the point (at some length, I have to say) that God made the world for his own pleasure and glory. That may sound selfish, but in fact, God is so perfectly selfless, that (a) he takes pure pleasure in the good of his creatures and (b) in doing so, he brings glory to himself. To express it slightly differently, at the heart of reality we find a God who is both perfectly satisfied in himself and who brings glory to himself by pouring his energies into people—creating and rescuing people like us. This is what this universe is for. This is what we are for. And that means that we are never more in step with God, perhaps we could even say more *God-like*, than when we are investing in others for their good, our joy, and God's glory.

The second step to joy, then, is to invest in other people. John Piper sums up the implications of this passage like this:

"We do not believe Jesus when he says there is more blessedness, more joy, more lasting pleasure in helping others than there is in a life devoted to our material comfort…" (*Desiring God*, p 100)

Questions for reflection

1. In which areas are you most likely to act in ways that don't fit with the gospel or that lack integrity?

2. Do you find real joy in other people?

3. What steps could you take to invest in others in a way which reflects the love which Christ has poured out on you?

PART TWO

We are midway through Paul's masterclass on how to be a joy-filled and joy-fuelled follower of the Lord Jesus Christ. His first two steps were to pursue integrity and to invest in people, which brings us to the third step.

Step 3: Say what needs to be said

Paul is committed to serving Christ with integrity, and he is determined to invest in people, including men like Titus and churches like that at Corinth. So it is hardly a surprise that he is also willing to say what needs to be said—even if it is deeply unpopular. Paul does this because he knows that this kind of loving honesty is a further step to sharing in real joy.

In 2 Corinthians **7:8**, Paul talks again about the difficult letter he has written to them. He has mentioned this several times, of course, but this time, Paul reveals that he knows how they responded to it: "For even if I made you grieve with my letter, I do not regret it—though I did regret it, for I see that that letter grieved you, though only for a while". Does he sound conflicted? A bit—but the message is clear. He didn't *want* to hurt them, but he knew it was better for them if he spoke the truth, painful though it was.

Chrysostom, living in the 4th century, wrote:

"Like a father who watches his son being operated on, Paul rejoices not for the pain being inflicted, but for the cure which is the ultimate result." 					(*Homilies. 2 Corinthians 15.1*)

And **Augustine**, slightly more colourfully, points out that even dung used in the right place in the right way leads to fruitfulness! (*Sermons for Easter* 254.4). Paul said what he had to, and the result was repentance and joy, both for him and for them (**7:9**). They were "grieved into repenting … For you felt a godly grief", and the result was joy.

So are you ready to put in a hard word when necessary? To say what needs to be said to bring people to their senses and bring them back to God? Are you ready to gently and lovingly call sin "sin" for the good of the church and for all involved? That is basically what Paul did in the "painful letter". He tackled a really difficult and messy moral issue in the church. And why did he do it? To make sure that it didn't drive a wedge down the middle of the church and damage the work of the gospel in the lives of these believers. He spells it out in **verse 12**—ultimately he wrote "in order that your earnestness for us might be revealed to you in the sight of God". He took the plunge and said what needed to be said, and the outcome was so healthy that he was encouraged (**v 13**). And the takeaway for us? Be prepared to say the hard thing—say what needs to be said.

I should just add a couple of caveats: first, do remember that you might be completely wrong; and second, don't expect people to thank you for your honesty—because they almost certainly won't, at least not straight away.

> Don't expect people to thank you for your honesty—they almost certainly won't.

We are people who instinctively blame others for our problems. That has a long and embarrassing history, stretching all the way back to Adam's conversation with God in Eden after he had sinned "because of the woman you put here". But there are also specific factors which make our generation particularly good at blaming other people.

I came across an old song on YouTube this week called "Psychiatric Folk Song" by an English woman called Anna Russell—it goes like this:

I went to my psychiatrist to be psychoanalyzed
To find out why I killed the cat and blacked my husband's eye.
He laid me on a downy couch to see what he could find,
And here's what he dredged up, from my subconscious mind.

When I was one, my mummy hid my dolly in a trunk
And so it follows, naturally, that I am always drunk.

When I was two, I saw my father kiss the maid one day,
And that is why I suffer from kleptomania.

At three I had a feeling of ambivalence towards my brothers,
And so it follows, naturally, I poisoned all my lovers.
But I am happy now I have learned the lessons this has taught:
Everything I do that's wrong is someone else's fault!

We need to remember that: straight talking, especially when it comes to our sinfulness, is rarely appreciated, not least because we are wired to blame someone else—but it is the third step to joy for gospel people.

Step 4: Seek joy through repentance

The final step to being a happy gospel worker is to seek joy through repentance, for the simple reason that godly grief leads to real repentance, which in turn leads to enjoying the freedom of our salvation in Christ. Or, to put it more bluntly, real repentance leads to joy.

Come with me to the verses at the heart of this section, which we have left basically untouched until now: "As it is, I rejoice, not because you were grieved, but because you were grieved into repenting. For you felt a godly grief, so that you suffered no loss through us" (**v 9-10**). The Corinthians felt the sting of Paul's words, they repented and they changed, and that brought him joy! Paul, however, isn't content to note what had happened—he wants to make a more general point, which is fundamental to the life of joy. He states the principle like this in **verse 10**: "For godly grief produces a repentance that leads to salvation without regret, whereas worldly grief produces death".

Paul then goes on in **verse 11** to detail the extent of the transformation that this godly repentance had brought about in the Corinthians—now they displayed a wholehearted "earnestness" and an "eagerness to clear yourselves", as well as "indignation" (basically a desire to do and to stand for what is right). This repentance also produced "fear" [of God] …"longing" (either for God or for reconciliation with Paul and the others), "zeal" and a concern for justice. Paul can even say that "at every point you have proved yourselves innocent in the matter". Real repentance has led to change and deep joy.

The stunning statement in verse 10, which lies at the heart of Paul's argument here, is vital for us unpack—for repentance is a much-neglected theme in contemporary evangelicalism. Paul writes, "For godly grief produces a repentance that leads to salvation without regret, whereas worldly grief produces death".

Repentance, properly understood, is the place to start the Christian life, and the place to stay, and the way to continue. In the words of writer Frederica Mathewes-Green:

> "Only repentance is brute-honest enough and joyous enough to bring us all the way home. But how repentance could be either joyous to us or vibrantly true is a foreign idea to most of us."
>
> (Quoted in George Guthrie, *2 Corinthians*, p 385)

And she's right. Repentance doesn't come easily to us. But it is the only thing that will bring us redemption, even restoration.

> Repentance doesn't come easily to us. But it is the only thing that will bring us redemption, even restoration.

You can see that in the distinction that Paul makes between "godly grief" and "worldly grief". Godly grief—literally grief "according to God"—leads to repentance and joy, and worldly grief leads to death. But what is he talking about? How can we tell the difference?

When life falls apart (and especially when we come face to face with our sin), we have a variety of options.

- Option A: "Crisis repentance"—the kind of thing that people do when the engines fail on the plane and they start making promises to a God whom, up until five seconds before, they refused to believe in.

- Option B: "Ritual repentance"—where we try to deal with our feelings of guilt by going to church at Christmas, or lighting a candle, or even giving some money to the rural fire brigade.

- Option C: "Manipulative repentance"—which is to put on a performance of despair, crying "Woe is me" as loudly and as often as necessary to elicit some sympathy from those around us, even if they happen to be the people we have hurt. If we pull that off, then we feel better, no further action is necessary and we can forget the whole thing.

The problem with options A, B and C is that they are all forms of "worldly grief", which leads, according to Paul, to *death*. So what kind of repentance is God looking for then?

Godly repentance is nowhere better (or more succinctly) expressed than in the Westminster Confession of Faith, published in London in 1646. Here's what it says:

"Repentance unto life is an evangelical **grace**, the doctrine whereof is to be preached by every minister of the Gospel, as well as that of faith in Christ. By it, a sinner, out of the sight and sense not only of the danger, but also of the filthiness and odiousness of his sins, as contrary to the holy nature, and righteous law of God; and upon the apprehension of His mercy in Christ to such as are penitent, so grieves for, and hates his sins, as to turn from them all unto God, purposing and endeavouring to walk with Him in all the ways of His commandments."

This is the way to relief and joy.

J. I. Packer sums this up memorably:

"Realistic recognition that we have wronged God
Regretful remorse at having dishonoured God
Reverent requesting of God's pardon
Resolute renunciation of sin
Requisite restitution to those we have hurt."

(*A Passion for Holiness,* p 123-135)

So eager is Packer to help us nail this that he adds an alternative al-literative series: "Discern the sin, desire forgiveness, decide to ask for help, deal with God, demonstrate change". But you get the point. When real repentance happens, we know. The tears are real, the words are humble, the determination is obvious, the change is real. And the joy is real. This is what flows from godly grief. This is "repentance unto life" (Acts 11:18, KJV). This is the repentance that leads to tears of relief and the sense of joy that flows to us through Jesus' death and resurrection.

As I write this, my adopted home of Australia is languishing under an overwhelming sense of national shame. Cricket is the most important sport in Australia, and our captain has just been caught cheating. He just looked so miserable and so sheepish as he tried to say that even though he cheated in a deliberate and premeditated way, he should continue as Australian captain. I can only imagine how terrible he feels as the nation bays for his blood. I wish that someone could explain to him that because of Jesus, there is not just pain but joy in repentance.

John Bunyan describes the joy of repentance like this:

"Christian ran thus till he came at a place somewhat ascending, and upon that place stood a Cross, and a little below, in the bottom, a Sepulchre. So I saw in my dream, That just as Christian came up with the Cross, his Burden loosed from off his shoulders, and fell from off his back, and began to tumble, and so continued to do, till it came to the mouth of the Sepulchre, where it fell in, and I saw it no more. Then was Christian glad and lightsome, and said with a merry heart, He has given me rest by His sorrow, and life by His death. Then he stood still a while to look and wonder; for it was very surprising to him, that the sight of the Cross should thus ease him of his Burden. He looked therefore, and looked again, even till the springs that were in his head sent the waters down his cheeks. Now, as he stood looking and weeping, behold three Shining Ones came to him and saluted him, with peace be to you; so the first said to him, Your sins are forgiven; the second stripped him of his rags, and clothed him with change of raiment; the third also set a Mark on his forehead, and gave him a Roll, with a Seal upon it, which bid him look on as he ran, and that he should give it in at the Celestial Gate; so they went their way. Then Christian gave three leaps of Joy, and went on singing…"

(The Pilgrim's Progress, p 53)

This is the joy of repentance. This is what we need for ourselves if we are to be godly, happy gospel workers, and this is what we should long for in others, because from this kind of repentance, from this kind of grief, according to God, flows real change and lasting joy.

The missing factor?

The challenge—and the encouragement—of this passage, then, is not complex. The way of joy is to pursue integrity, give ourselves to people, say what needs to be said, speak gospel truth into our own lives and the lives of others, and look for, long for, repentance which leads to joy and transformation through the gospel, as God does his work both in and through us.

Let me leave you to reflect on one last question. Which of these factors is missing for you? Integrity? Love? The courage to speak? Repentance that leads to life? Joy? Whatever it is—the answer, the strength we need, the forgiveness, the willpower, the delight, all of it— is already ours in the Lord Jesus Christ: the one who both embodies and provides the real deal when it comes to joy—the happiness of God himself.

Men and women who, in the Lord Jesus, have found true and lasting joy through the gospel, the announcement that Jesus died and rose again, can point others to that joy in the strength that he alone supplies.

Questions for reflection

1. Why do we find it so hard to say hard things to people, even to people we love? Why should we do it?

2. Do you consider repentance to be a part of your life? How could you make it part of your daily walk as a Christian?

3. Why do we settle for shallow apologies rather than the tears and joys of godly sorrow that brings repentance?

8. GIVE LIKE A MACEDONIAN

So far in this letter, Paul has put it all out there—his passion for Christ and the gospel, his convictions about ministry, his concern for the church family in Corinth, his heart for individuals, his fears for their long-term future and even his delight in their repentance after his last awkward letter. So having done all that, what's left? It's time to *talk about money.* In chapters 8 and 9, Paul gives us the longest, most rigorous, most sustained treatment of a gospel-shaped attitude to money in the whole Bible—and why does he do it? *Because he needed it.*

It's easy to forget that these letters aren't abstract theoretical treatises laying out the theological foundation for Christianity—although they do exactly that, of course. They are *real letters*, written for pressing and urgent reasons—in this case, to get the prosperous Corinthians to part with large amounts of their hard-earned cash so that their poor brothers and sisters back in Jerusalem could put some food on their table. Paul wrote to get the Corinthians to make sure that when Titus and his friends showed up, there would be a large pile of coins waiting for them.

However, in tackling this slightly embarrassing issue, Paul gives us a stunning model of applying the gospel to a real-world, real-time situation. And as he does this, it becomes apparent that while money is the presenting issue, for Paul, these chapters are basically a call to be open-hearted, wholehearted, gospel-hearted followers of Jesus— which will, of course, show in the way they handle their money. So strap yourselves in and get a firm grip on your wallet, as we look at these two chapters in five broad movements.

Gospel generosity

For Paul, there is absolutely no doubt that *the gospel produces generosity.* If he had needed convincing of that, then the churches of Macedonia (**8:1**)—Philippi, Thessalonica and Berea—had done a great job. It seems that these local churches, despite significant struggles, had blown the apostle away with their selfless generosity, which he knows can only come from the grace of God.

> The Macedonians understood that giving is a delight, and even an expression of joy.

According to **verses 2-3**, their giving was clearly *sacrificial*—Paul says they actually gave more than they could afford, as their "extreme poverty … overflowed in a wealth of generosity", as they "gave according to their means … and beyond their means". It was remarkably enthusiastic—they *begged* Paul *earnestly* for the privilege of getting involved in the collection he was organising for the struggling church in Jerusalem. And it was also deeply *spiritual*—despite the fact that they were under financial pressure, "their abundance of joy … overflowed in a wealth of generosity". They understood that giving is a delight, and *even an expression of joy*.

The idea of joyful giving is a strange concept for most of us. I have been in African churches where people dance up to the front to bring their offerings—but in most other churches I've been in, there seems to be a competition to see how quickly we can move an empty bag or plate from the back to the front, with no one acting as if anything significant, let alone joyful, is happening. But for the Macedonians, when it was time for the offering, gasps of "Oh yes" could be heard from every part of the room. They actually begged to be allowed to give (**v 4**). That's because they knew that giving to other believers (and the work of the gospel through Paul) was the overflow of the fact that they "gave themselves first to the Lord and then by the will of God to us" (**v 5**).

It's a startling sentence. This is why, ultimately, this passage isn't just about money—it's about living for Jesus. Does this simple statement sum up where you've got to in your **discipleship**? "They gave themselves first to the Lord and then by the will of God to us" (v 5). It's very straightforward at one level, but it reveals a depth of commitment and seriousness that we'd do well to copy—for this was the source of their generosity. They gave themselves to God—they committed themselves wholeheartedly in repentance and faith, and so they gave themselves to one another, and as a result, they gave away their money.

In his commentary on this passage, Calvin makes the profound observation that our problem is that we think something is *lost* when we give it away—especially when we give it to other people. The Macedonians had been freed up by the gospel, and so they realised that to give is to gain, not to lose, even in their poverty.

That's why Paul tells the Corinthians to give like Macedonians, and he sends Titus, who had first raised the possibility of a collection with them, to see it through (**v 6**), adding in **verse 7**, probably slightly tongue in cheek, "But as you excel in everything—in faith, in speech, in knowledge, in all earnestness, and in our love for you—see that you excel in this act of grace also". In 1 Corinthians, Paul had plenty to say about the Corinthians' propensity to talk themselves up. Now he says that they have an opportunity to put their money where their mouth is—for the gospel produces generosity, *so give like Macedonians*.

Now I have no doubt that Paul's words must have made them squirm just a little. There is hardly a nation in the world which doesn't have some issues with their neighbours. It must have irked them just a little to be told to be like Macedonians—it is a bit like being asked, "Why can't you be more like your sister?" But the beauty of the gospel is that it helps us to get over our pride and our ego to recognise what God has done through the gospel in other people, to learn from them and be spurred on by them.

Incidentally, that's why it's so anti-gospel to act as if we have all the answers. We should be asking constantly, in every situation: "What can I learn from you?" City churches should look at regional churches and ask themselves: "What have we to learn?" Native churches should look at ethnic churches and ask: "What have they got that we haven't?" American churches should look at churches in China and Thailand and Japan, and ask: "Where do they live and speak the gospel in ways that we don't?" **Reformed** churches should look at **charismatic** churches, **credobaptists** should look at **paedobaptists** and vice-versa and ask: "What can we learn?" We should do it because, as Paul says, the *grace of God has been given* to God's people *everywhere*.

After telling them to give like Macedonians, in 8:8-15, Paul raises the stakes just a little—he looks for...

Gospel sacrifice like Jesus

Not only does the gospel produce generosity; it also produces *selflessness*. This seems to be Paul's point in **verse 8**, where he encourages his readers to be sacrificial. "to prove by the earnestness of others that your love also is genuine". Paul's tone here is persuasive rather than commanding—not least because, as we shall see, things are rarely black and white when it comes to money. But his main concern is that the Corinthians would display real selflessness, which would lead to the strengthening of others. (The ESV has the word "earnestness", but something like "spiritual health" or "zeal" might be better.) That's why he pulls out his biggest theological gun at this point and tells them to act like Jesus (**v 9**):

> "For you know the grace of our Lord Jesus Christ, that though he was rich, yet for your sake he became poor, so that you by his poverty might become rich."

In one brief phrase, Paul gathers together the pre-existence of the Son, the grace which God has shown us in the **incarnation**, and Jesus' death in our place. And this rich and powerful combination is called into service to urge the Corinthians to be selfless and to add to the collection for their poor brothers and sisters. In particular, they need to make sure they follow through on their pledges.

In the same way that Jesus followed through for our sake, so we are to follow through on our commitments for the sake of others. So if you say you are going to support someone financially as they take the gospel to another people group, then go and fill out the forms and set up the direct debit. If you say you're going to pray for someone, do it then and there, or add them to your prayer list. If you say you are going to show up to help set out the chairs, then make sure you are there. Follow through on your commitments. Why? Because Jesus did.

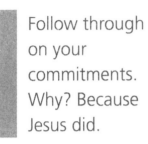

Follow through on your commitments. Why? Because Jesus did.

It's pretty clear that a year earlier, the Corinthians had made encouraging noises about supporting the Jerusalem Fund. Now they need to come up with the cash. Now was the moment when they needed to prioritise others and open their wallets.

In the verses that follow, Paul continues to fill out a robust Christian approach to giving. And he starts right here, as he insists that as followers of Jesus, we need to be people who follow through on our commitments. In **verses 10-11**, he reminds them of their pledge a year earlier, and tells them to follow through now. *If you commit, then do it.* That's a mark of Christian character, or perhaps a *virtue*, where virtue is shorthand for settled, godly, consistent habits. I hope you can see that following through on our commitments is actually an index of Christ-like selflessness.

You may not have thought about it like this, but usually—perhaps almost always—it is "self" which gets in the way of us doing what we have committed to. I don't do what I have told you I would do because I have prioritised something which is more important to myself. That may not be very flattering, but it's true. If I make you a promise, and then fail to deliver, it will almost certainly be because I have prioritised myself before you, which is selfish, and the very antithesis of Christ-likeness. In other words, it was all about me. I wanted something else more. That's why Paul urges the Corinthians to display a selflessness which is generated and maintained by the gospel, and to follow through on what they have promised.

Paul, however, committed as he is to raising this money, goes to great lengths to make it crystal clear that giving is to be *voluntary* and *proportionate*—that is, it is acceptable according to what a person has, not according to what he does not have (**verse 12**). Paul's ideal is that Christian believers would *choose* to put others first, caring for each other when they can—in a kind of grace-driven equilibrium, where everyone is looking out for other people. It's worth quoting the principle in full from **verses 13-14**:

> "For I do not mean that others should be eased and you burdened, but that as a matter of fairness your abundance at the present time should supply their need, so that their abundance may supply your need, that there may be fairness."

When I need help, you help me; when you need help, I help you. Nobody is keeping score, but there is a natural ebb and flow as we live together in dependence, without either shame, which would stop us asking for help, or greed, which would stop us giving it. When I have more than enough, I gladly help you, and you do the same back.

The principle of "taking enough" is then supported from Exodus 16:18, which Paul quotes in 2 Corinthians **9:15**. Remember the way in which it worked with manna in the wilderness? There was a spiritual law of diminishing returns. Or, if I can put it like this, *excess is toxic*. Calvin again comments:

> "Those who have riches, whether inherited or won by their own industry and labour, are to remember that what is left over is meant, not for **intemperance** or luxury, but for relieving the needs of the brethren." *(Commentary on 2nd Corinthians*, p 114)

Wow—that stings, doesn't it? And it clearly reveals just how counter-cultural this all is.

We often run on the principle that we work hard so that we can play hard. Our default is that we spend as much as we can afford on ourselves. Paul says that the way of the gospel, the way of Christ, is to lavish whatever we can on others for the sake of the gospel. It's to give like a Macedonian and to give things up for the sake of Jesus and others.

Questions for reflection

1. What stops us giving more generously?

2. According to Paul, what is the ultimate reason for giving *sacrificially*? What does sacrificial giving look like?

3. Who and what should we give to?

PART TWO

Gospel service

In **8:16**, Paul continues his discussion of gospel-shaped generosity. The gospel also produces *servant-heartedness*. How does this show itself? In Titus putting his hand up to go to Corinth to collect their part of the money, but also in the depth of care he shows to them (**v 16-17**). He went above and beyond to serve them, as did the two other brothers mentioned in verses 18-23.

Paul doesn't tell us their names, but that's probably explained by the fact that when the letter was read in the churches in Achaia, these men would have been standing at the front (perhaps even reading it out). I don't think there is anything odd going on here. Paul just doesn't mention their names because that isn't the point. The point is that, along with Titus, these two men are committed to serving others in and through the gospel. One of them is actually famous among all the churches for his preaching of the gospel (**v 18**). Wouldn't that be a great way to be remembered? This party of three was appointed by the "churches" (**v 19**)—presumably the key churches in Macedonia— to make sure that the gift was received, so the church in Jerusalem would be encouraged and God himself glorified. They did it all "for the glory of the Lord himself and to show our good will" (perhaps better "readiness to help" is better). Which leads to the key principle of **verses 20-21**.

For Paul it is an absolute non-negotiable that things are done properly—that is, in a way which brings honour to God, and also, which doesn't drag the church needlessly into disrepute. He sums up his approach in verse 21: "We aim at what is honourable not only in the Lord's sight but also in the sight of man". Why is he so passionate about this? Because he knows that fights and accusations about money will kill off gospel ministry more quickly than almost anything else. When it comes to money, we need to be beyond reproach, because only then will people be able to see that the gospel produces genuine servant-heartedness.

Now, of course, this is a little tricky to put into practice. It's easy to take these words and adopt them for precisely the opposite reason to Paul's. For Paul, it's all about ensuring that *nothing hinders the gospel,* and in particular, that nothing obscures the fact that we serve other people for the sake of Christ. We, however, are very sinful and are more than capable of pouring our efforts into being recognised as honourable for our own sake. Welcome to the human race! There is no easy solution to that one, other than to double our vigilance and throw ourselves in weakness on the One who will help us to live in a way which says "We are about Christ, not ourselves". Paul has sounded this note repeatedly in this letter (e.g. 4:5)—which happens to be exactly what anonymous brother number two was known for.

Here's what Paul writes about him in **8:22**: he is the one:

"… whom we have often tested and found earnest [or zealous, or spiritually healthy] in many matters, but who is now more earnest [or zealous] than ever because of his great confidence in you."

Paul is sending helper number two because he is so committed to the welfare of the Corinthians. Now remember, the Corinthians aren't exactly the easiest or the most consistent bunch—and yet Titus and his friends are absolutely committed to them—Paul sums this up in **verses 23-24**:

"As for Titus, he is my partner and fellow worker for your benefit. And as for our brothers, they are messengers [apostles] of the churches, the glory of Christ."

That is, they are bringing glory to Christ.

This is the kind of servant-heartedness we are called to and equipped for in the gospel. Unfortunately, our serving doesn't always come with the requisite humility attached. It's more than possible to trumpet the fact that we are serving in church. But I think we know, in our heart of hearts, whether we are serving God and others, or ourselves.

And how are the Corinthians to respond to men like this coming to them? Not to put too fine a point on it, Paul says, *Show me the money* (**v 24**). It's time for them to come through for Paul and his team and for the church in Jerusalem. I hope you can see what Paul is doing here—he is calling them to give like Macedonians, to live selflessly like Jesus; he then holds out to them the servant-heartedness of Titus and the anonymous two—and he is doing it all for the sake of the church. Paul is giving the Corinthians every reason he can think of to love one another in the gospel.

Gospel integrity

But he isn't quite finished yet—in 9:1-5, we see that the gospel also produces *integrity*. In these verses, Paul doesn't actually do much more than call on them to do the right thing. Paul knows they know what they need to do—and now they need to get on and do it (**verses 1-2**). The Macedonians have been encouraged by the Corinthians' loud pledges to send money to Jerusalem—but now, it has come down to the wire. The Corinthians either have to come up with the money, or there will be humiliation all round, as Paul's boasting about them will prove "empty in this matter" (**v 3**, and he says the same thing in different words in **v 4**). So Paul has gone out on a limb and made arrangements for the money to be collected and delivered, "so that it may be ready as a willing gift, not as an exaction". The last phrase can be translated as "not as an expression of stinginess". The gift is to be free, generous, and ready when Titus gets there.

It is said that, in ancient Greece, benefactors who didn't make good on their pledge would have their names published in the **Agora** in Athens, to inflict suitable humiliation on them—much like the "naming and shaming" culture of today. I'm reminded of the church committee meeting I was at about 30 years ago when someone suggested that the giving would go up if we published all the names and amounts of the giving in the previous 12 months! Paul doesn't go that far, but it is clear that for him that the failure of the Corinthians to come through on their word would be a very big deal indeed. Again, he puts his reputation and relationship on the line here—if they fail to keep their promise, then they will be shaming Paul, who had trusted their word and made promises to others on their behalf. Underneath this however is the principle that the gospel produces integrity. God has spoken to us reliably and kept every promise he makes, so we need to make every effort to speak reliably to others. Integrity matters.

> When it comes to spiritual leadership, nothing is more foundational than integrity.

When it comes to spiritual leadership, nothing is more foundational than integrity. We have to deliver on our promises. We have to do what we say. We have to be consistent. We have to be principled. None of us are perfect, and people will forgive mistakes, but where the pattern of our lives is one of saying one thing and doing another—where we don't come through on our grand plans and commitments—our spiritual authority will quickly be corroded from within, and we will be left in a place from which it is very hard to recover. So what are we to do? To live a life of integrity that is made possible for us only through the gospel itself.

And finally, in 9:6-15, Paul gathers up his argument and intensifies it even further as he homes in again on gospel giving.

Gospel giving

First, in **verses 6-7**, Paul tells the Corinthians to give not because they are guilted into it, or pressured into producing their credit card, but because God just loves a happy giver. The basic principle is laid out in **verse 6**: "Whoever sows sparingly will also reap sparingly, and whoever sows bountifully will also reap bountifully". This is what lies behind the obligation-free, pain-free encouragement to share resources in **verse 7**, where we are encouraged to give *thoughtfully* and neither "reluctantly [nor] under compulsion". Why? Simply because "God loves a cheerful giver". We tend to live by a different and more worldly proverb: *God gives credit to a reluctant but careful giver*. Paul seems to have something a little freer, a little more lavish, in mind. When it comes to giving, extravagance is good!

The little-known 5th-century theologian Maximus of Turin wrote these words:

"Joyful and cheerful then is one who attends to the poor. Quite clearly, he is joyful, because for a few small coins he acquires heavenly treasures for himself; on the contrary, the person who pays taxes is always sad and dejected. Rightly is he sad who is not drawn to payment by love but forced by fear. Christ's debtor then is joyful and Caesar's sad, because love urges the one to payment and punishment constrains the other; the one is invited by rewards, the other compelled by penalties."

(Quoted in Gerald Bray, *1, 2 Corinthians Volume 7,* p 280)

> Be a bit more reckless in your giving, and have a good laugh about it as you give.

So let me urge you to be a bit more reckless in your giving, and to have a good laugh about it as you give. Metaphorically, dance your way up to the front with a broad smile on your face every time you have the opportunity to give. And when we can't give, let's make sure we see it as missing out! We'll be sad not because we've had to part with our hard-earned pennies but because we have missed out on great joy from God himself!

The fact is that people who show gospel generosity, selfless sacrifice, servant-heartedness and integrity *never, ever* miss out! Look at what Paul says in **verse 8**: "And God is able to make all grace abound to you". That is, God has the ability to lavish on you every kind of grace. And Paul doesn't stop there: he insists that "having all sufficiency in all things at all times, you may abound in every good work"—a principle which he backs up with a quotation in **verse 9** from Psalm 112:9. The kind of gospel-shaped life that leads us to give cheerfully and generously will put us in a great place, for God will continue to supply us with *whatever we need* to get on with the work of the gospel right here, right now.

Our God loves to drench us with good things, which Paul describes metaphorically in 2 Corinthians **9:10** as multiplying "your seed for sowing and increasing the harvest of your righteousness". God will give us all the resources we need to grow ourselves and to support our brothers and sisters. Paul is quoting Isaiah 55:10—where God's word does not return to him without accomplishing what it was designed for—and Hosea 10:12, with its harvest of righteousness. These Old Testament allusions show that Paul has now moved far beyond finance to the way in which God works in and through the gospel, transforming people like us and driving us to share the truth and love of the gospel). 2 Corinthians **9:11** takes it even further: "You will be enriched in every way to be generous in every way". This is what the gospel does in us: in the gospel God lavishes his gifts on us and frees us up to pass on the same precious gift to other people…

Now it's important to be very clear on the fact that God does not give any blanket guarantees of either wealth or health to his people. The so called "**prosperity gospel**" is a pernicious evil and a blight on the church. It routinely promises what God does not, and overreaches, blaming its failures on the very people it has defrauded. The challenge for those of us who have been sucked into thinking like this is to bring our expectations and demands for this life back into line with what God has actually promised.

But for many of us, I suspect that the danger is not that we expect *too much* from God here and now but *too little*. We are far too cynical to need our expectations dampened with a healthy dose of biblical realism. So what do we need? We need to expect more—we need to take God seriously when he says:

"He who supplies seed to the sower and bread for food will supply and multiply your seed for sowing and increase the harvest of your righteousness.....You will be enriched in every way to be generous in every way." (**v 10-11**)

We can afford to give: to give generously—to give with a broad grin on our faces—because when we do that, we demonstrate that we know and trust the God who has promised to do us nothing but good. It isn't that we give and God gives back to us, or that he gives more, or anything like that. Our giving demonstrates that we believe the gospel and trust God to do us good, in riches or poverty.

And what's the net result of all this? In **verse 12** Paul says, "Through us [your generosity] will produce thanksgiving to God". All this selfless giving of every kind won't just meet the needs of God's people; it is producing (and will produce) "many thanksgivings to God". Gospel giving flows out of gratitude, and then multiplies gratitude, which, of course, leads to a display and recognition of God's glory,. Paul highlights this in **verse 13**: "By their approval of this ministry, they will glorify God". Their submission to the will of God, which flows from their "confession of the gospel of Christ", is expressed both in "the generosity of your contribution [fellowship] for them and for all others", and (**v 14**) their love and prayers for God's people: "...while they long for you and pray for you, because of the surpassing grace of God upon you". When the Corinthians express their submission to Christ by coming up with the money, all will be well. The solid commitment that they have shown will spill over into prayer, as God's people cry together, "Thanks be to God for his inexpressible gift!" (**v 15**). God has given grace to us; we give in response to the gospel and in the power of the gospel, knowing that generosity is only ever for our good and the glory of Jesus.

Embrace the gospel!

We are called to be generous, sacrificial, servant-hearted and morally completely dependable—but at every stage, Paul calls us to do this by *embracing the gospel.* Why should the Corinthians give to Jerusalem? Because of what God has done for them and is doing in them and will do in the Lord Jesus Christ. Because of the Macedonians. Because of Christ. Because of Titus' servant-heartedness. Because of their own need for integrity. Because it's clear everywhere they look that the gospel helps us to see the true value of things, and frees us up from our attachment to things, and breaks the chains of our self-preoccupation and our fears for the future, and creates a deep love and concern for others. We do not need to fret because our God is utterly committed to our flourishing and the progress of the gospel—so we can give and live with a broad grin on our faces. So let's thank God for his inexpressible gift to us in the gospel of the Lord Jesus Christ, because it really does make all the difference in the world.

Questions for reflection

1. How do you think your friends would describe you in relation to money?

2. Gospel integrity matters enormously. Why?

3. Giving, according to Paul, is both good for us and promotes God's glory. How do these two work together?

9. THE ELEPHANT IN THE ROOM

In 1814, Ivan Andreevich Krylov, poet and author, wrote a fable entitled *The Inquisitive Man,* which tells of a man who goes to a museum and notices all sorts of tiny things, but fails to notice an elephant. Fyodor Dostoevsky, in his novel *Demons,* wrote, "Belinsky was just like Krylov's Inquisitive Man, who didn't notice the elephant in the museum". From there, the "elephant in the museum" went on a linguistic walkabout, eventually becoming domesticated as "the elephant in the room"—a phrase which aptly sums up the issue that Paul is addressing in 2 Corinthians 10.

Now you may have noticed something strange about the story so far. Up to this point, Paul has made no direct reference to the people who lie at the source of the problems in his relationship with the church. He hasn't mentioned those who showed up after his first extended church-planting visit to Corinth, and who caused all kinds of problems (reflected, for example, in 1 Corinthians 1:10-2:5). But now, as he moves to the conclusion of his letter, it's time to turn to the very large, impressive-sounding, philosophically sophisticated, personally vitriolic elephant in the room. In 2 Corinthians 10, Paul finally tackles the specific and damaging accusations which have been levelled against him with devastating effect by these deeply divisive, theologically misguided and thoroughly arrogant self-styled "Christian philosophers".

There are few harder things to cope with—and few things of which we can be more certain if we are followers of Jesus—than personal attack. Sometimes people will question our convictions. At other times they will undermine our character. At other times still they may pour scorn on our competencies. They might even do all three at once. Some of the time their attacks will be outrageous. Some of the time they will be more subtle. Some of the time they will be perfectly justified. At other times, they will be completely spurious. Often, criticisms and attacks will be a mixture of truth and lies. But whatever the nature of the attacks, they will come, and we will need to be ready—ready to listen, ready to learn, ready to refute lies, ready to change course, ready to be corrected, ready to stand firm.

So how do we know which to do? How do we get the balance between refusing to yield on the gospel and being defensive? Between being open to correction and weakly compromising on the gospel? How on earth do we navigate this minefield? We could do much worse than watch how Paul does it, as he follows in the footsteps of the Lord Jesus himself.

Paul's response to his opponents—the way in which he handles opposition and difficulties—is marked by seven principles which, I think, provide an excellent approach to negotiating the highly emotional relational complexities that are part and parcel of life in the church and, in particular, go with the territory when it comes to Christian leadership. Paul's "seven habits of extremely godly leaders under attack" are at times startling, at times predictable and at times deeply reassuring.

Habit 1: Be meek and gentle

For most of this letter, Paul has written on behalf of his whole team—but not now. Now he steps forward into the glare of the spotlight and says, "I, Paul, myself entreat you, by the meekness and gentleness of Christ" (**10:1**). Apparently, the accusation levelled at Paul was that he was a roaring lion when he was miles away with a pen in his hand, but a little lamb when he actually showed up. That's reflected in the second half of the verse: "I who am humble when face to face with you, but bold towards you when I am away!" The Corinthians were accusing him of double standards, which is often the first "go to" for anyone wanting to criticise. But in this case his opponents, it seems, had got things very wrong indeed.

In the first place, his opponents had completely misunderstood the gospel. They thought that to call someone "humble" was the ultimate insult. It's sad really, for in saying that, they showed that they had completely missed the point of the gospel.

It was a very Greek issue—in fact it's the same basic issue that dominated much of 1 Corinthians, where the message of the cross was viewed as too stupid for words. Now, however, it isn't the message itself that's under fire but the messenger. And Paul's response? He counters their ridiculous, wrong-headed accusations with Christ-like poise and strength. He fights their fire with "meekness" (see also Matthew 5:5; Philippians 4:5). They attacked him. He appealed to the Corinthians with meekness and gentleness. This isn't always the picture we have of Paul, but it seems that he was slow to take offence, ready to put up with accusations and always committed to putting others first. He was gentle.

> Paul was slow to take offence, ready to put up with accusations and always committed to putting others first.

Paul has been working for *years* to see this church plant in Corinth flourish. He has seen all his work undermined and his reputation dismantled by these unnamed itinerant teachers, who have carved out a living for themselves as the new thing on the old philosophy circuit. But how does he respond when they try to take him down? In the same way that Jesus himself responded to those who were plotting to kill him. In a controlled, gracious, gentle way. Is that easy? Of course not—but this is the change that the gospel brings about in people like us. The Spirit produces real-time fruit in our lives, enabling us to live and speak like Jesus himself, even when we are attacked. *The gentleness that Christ himself showed, he asks of us and enables us to live out.*

So is gentleness the dominant note of your life? Even when you're attacked? It should be. It can be. Paul Tripp explains it like this:

> "When you experience these deficiencies in your fellow believers, do you respond with a wrecking-ball attitude of condemnation? Are you quick to knock them down and destroy their character? Or are you gentle in your reaction … You see, gentleness will not come naturally to you. Sin has turned your heart into a wrecking ball. But remember, you're never alone. There's grace for your struggle. Jesus is with you, Jesus is for you, and Jesus is in you."*

That's the first habit we need to develop if we are to respond well to personal attacks.

Habit 2: Trust the truth

We mustn't make the mistake of thinking that Paul's commitment to acting and reacting like Christ (with meekness and gentleness) made him a soft touch, because it's equally clear that he has a deep passion for the truth of the gospel, which drives everything he says in this mess. He refuses to make it about him and makes sure that God's work in our world through the gospel stays front and centre. He trusts the truth to do its work.

Incredibly, Paul's opponents were accusing him of being unspiritual—of "walking according to the flesh" (**10:2**). Paul longs not to have to confront those who are undermining him—although, if he has to, he will. *Why?* Because this really matters. It's not really about him at all; the real issue is the nature of true gospel ministry. Is the super-spiritual, super-impressive, super-confident psycho-babble of the sophisticates the real thing? Not according to Paul, whose down-to-earth ministry of the gospel can hardly be more different. He may not be all that impressive, but his ministry—gospel ministry—is the

---

* www.paultripp.com/wednesdays-word/posts/walk-with-gentleness, accessed 2/7/18

real thing. Look how he spells that out from **verse 3**: "For though we walk in the flesh [*yes, we are frail, finite human beings*], we are not waging war according to the flesh". The picture Paul uses in these verses is almost certainly that of a Roman siege engine, which, after smashing down the walls surrounding a city and even the inner citadel, enables the invading armies to pour through the walls, taking prisoners and punishing those who persist in rebelling against the new rulers. And this is how the gospel operates. The gospel weapons we deploy (**v 4**) "have divine power to destroy strongholds". And what are these weapons? Essentially, Paul uses gospel proclamation (**v 5**) to "destroy arguments and every lofty opinion raised against the knowledge of God, and take every thought captive to obey Christ".

If Paul is meek and gentle when attacked personally, when it comes to truth, he is passionate and fearless! Unlike his opponents, who are always trying to accommodate the gospel to existing philosophical ideas, Paul is happy to unleash the power of the gospel on those very ideas with devastating effects. He is committed to "taking every thought captive to Christ", that is, to bringing the truth to bear in the public square, exposing every human philosophy for what it is. Such is the power of the gospel that it will bring both salvation and judgment: "being ready to punish every disobedience, when your obedience is complete" (**v 6**). Paul's personal frailty may be obvious, but so is the power of the gospel. Paul's opponents can say what they like about him, but Paul will not let them deny the fact that his ministry, because it is *gospel* ministry, has real spiritual power.

The irony is that while his opponents make it personal, Paul knows it is all about the gospel. He refuses to play the player rather than the ball. They say that he is worldly and that they are deeply spiritual. Paul shows the reverse is true by focusing on what they haven't grasped— that when God works, he does so freely and graciously through the gospel by the power of the Spirit in broken people like us, rather than through human giftedness. The evidence that his unimpressive, humble, "as a dying man to dying men" ministry is the real thing is not his giftedness but the fact that the gospel changes people, and takes on powerful empires and ideas and brings them to their knees. For Paul, it's not about him; it's about the gospel.

The problem is, of course, that it's very easy to say that it's not personal, and very hard to believe it, and to keep believing it. I don't know if you've experienced that yet—but if you are involved in serving Christ for any length of time, you will. At times, you will be deeply tempted to think that it really is all about you. This has been a danger for people like us since the beginning (see for example Deuteronomy 8:11-18). We must do everything in our power to remember that we never get past needing God to work in us (and through us) *by his grace*. God always works by grace all the time. A day will never come when we can say, "I am now wise, and God works because of me rather than in spite of me". We must not trust ourselves but only the truth of the gospel.

Calvin wrote this deeply arresting statement:

"For nothing is more opposed to the spiritual wisdom of God than the wisdom of the flesh, and nothing is more opposed to his grace than man's natural ability, and it is the same with everything the world thinks exalted. Thus the abasement of man is the only foundation of the Kingdom of Christ."

(*Commentary on 2 Corinthians*, p 130)

This is a profound insight: *nothing is more opposed to God's grace than man's natural ability.* We cannot be confident in ourselves and in God at the same time. We cannot live by grace while robbing God of glory and giving ourselves the credit. We cannot be passionate about the truth while defending our own reputation. Paul gets that exactly right—he is utterly convinced of both his own weakness, and the power of the gospel, and he lives out of both.

> We cannot be confident in ourselves and in God at the same time.

That's why he is so passionate about the truth. And that's what comes out when he is attacked.

Habit 3: Put your confidence in Christ

Paul's attackers were very confident that they were "in Christ"—and seemingly they weren't so sure about Paul. The apostle's reply is in 2 Corinthians **10:7-8**. He urges the Corinthians to recognise what's staring them in the face: "If anyone is confident that he is Christ's, let him remind himself that just as he is Christ's, so also are we". Paul is quite happy to assert that he has been joined by faith to Christ, and that this permanent, irreversible reality is the bedrock both of his own security and his ministry. But his confidence in Christ stretches beyond that. He goes on to say that, at times, his confidence may even have looked a bit like boasting, but as God himself has given him the responsibility of "building you up and not … destroying you", he won't shy away from that.

We have already seen multiple times in this letter that, for Paul, boasting in Christ is not a bad thing—in fact it reflects a host of healthy spiritual realities: we will only boast in Christ if we trust him implicitly, and believe that he really does have the power to change people through the gospel. In this context, we believe that Christ re-cruits and commissions leaders like Paul to wield spiritual authority in the church. So for Paul, his boasting was the direct result of the fact that God had already brought people in Corinth to new life in Christ, and had given him the direct responsibility for leading and nurturing this church family. Paul, then, was confident in both his salvation in Christ, and his commissioning by Christ as an apostle to the Gentiles. That meant that when the heat came on, he was more than able to withstand it.

There will be times for all of us, if we keep going, when we have to say to ourselves, "I know I am broken, sinful and inconsistent—but I am in Christ, and he has appointed me to serve him; so I'm going to get on with it whatever people think of me, in the strength that he supplies". That's what it means to put our confidence in Christ—and that, believe it or not, is both freeing and empowering.

For a start, it protects us from being too confident in ourselves. Self-confidence and self-righteousness damage us and the church, and make us a pain to be around. Spurgeon once said this:

"I cannot make out what has happened to some of my brethren who fancy themselves so wonderfully good. I wish the Lord would strip them of their self-righteousness and let them see themselves as they really are in his sight. Their fine notions concerning the higher life would soon vanish then."

(Quoted by D. A. Carson in *From Triumphalism and Maturity,* p 65)

But putting our confidence in Christ also energises us to get on with the great task of taking the gospel to our world! The mindset we must cultivate is that *we can't do anything—but Christ can and will!* And it's this confidence—this boast—which enabled Paul to keep going, and which will enable us to keep going, even when the pressure is great.

Questions for reflection

1. How do you normally react when you are attacked? How is it possible for people like you and me to respond like Jesus instead?

2. Why is it so hard to put our own hurt or reputation aside for the sake of the gospel?

3. If we are "in Christ", what difference does that make to the way in which we cope under pressure?

PART TWO

Habit 4: Commit to consistency

The fourth principle of Paul's response isn't really a response at all—in that it's something that marked Paul's ministry from the start to the end. It doesn't sound particularly profound, but it is very, very significant. It's *consistency*. The last thing Paul wanted to do was to freak people out with his letters (**10:9**). And even though he had been accused of being a bit of a letdown in the flesh, with both his physique and his **oratory** being very unimpressive (**v 10**), Paul makes the point that with him, *what you see is what you get*. In **verse 11**, he states simply, "What we say by letter when absent, we do when present".

The accusation that was levelled against him was a tough one. It's basically that he was duplicitous—writing one thing and saying another face to face. It's like being really straight in emails, confronting of all kinds of sin directly, but then wimping out of every difficult or uncomfortable personal conversation face to face. That kind of contradiction will slowly but surely kill our usefulness, as gradually our actions undermine our words. Thankfully, Paul was able to say, on the basis of multiple previous visits to the city of Corinth, that this just wasn't true. With Paul, you got the same person one to one as you did in his letters or at the front on Sundays. He lived a joined-up life. Which raises the very obvious question, do we?

The trouble is that most of us tend to shy away from awkward conversations. We don't like confronting or accusing people, or making others people feel bad. Add to that the fact that in many cultures today, the overwhelming demand is that we exercise *tolerance* in every relationship and every situation, and it becomes very difficult to have any kind of hard conversations one to one.

The problem is that if we give up loving honesty and consistency for the sake of being tolerant, it leaves us wide open to the very kind of accusation levelled at Paul. That's why together in this generation and every generation, we need to pursue the kind of consistency that marked Jesus' dealings with people, and Paul's. Whatever the situation, whatever the cost, Paul spoke the gospel into people's lives. Is that me? Is that you? God calls us to this kind of joined-up life, so that when trouble comes, nobody can say that we are changing our story to suit ourselves. Let's be consistent.

Habit 5: Don't compare

A few years ago, I went with a friend to watch his young son play football. The hilarious thing, Mike explained, was that this was *non-competitive* soccer. Apparently, the idea of winning and losing was just too much for these seven-year-olds to deal with. So there would be no winners and losers, every game would be a draw and no one would keep score. Except that no one had told the kids about this, and they greeted each goal with a carefully choreographed team celebration and such strictly non-competitive comments as "6-1", "I've scored 5!" and "We're stuffing you". But Paul, it seems, really did operate in a non-competitive environment. Even though his opponents were clearly into comparison, he wasn't (2 Corinthians **10:12**): "But when they measure themselves by one another and compare themselves with one another, they are without understanding [literally, *completely clueless*]". According to the first part of the verse, Paul isn't going to have anything to do with that kind of nonsense.

Comparing ourselves with other people when it comes to gospel ministry really is appalling. In fact, it shows we have completely lost the gospel plot. And yet we do it. We look at someone else and say to ourselves, "How come people seem to like them better than me?" "How come she treats her better than me?" "How come they get better grades/get paid more than me?" And so it goes on. And unfortunately, it's the kind of thing that church leaders slip into: "I'm smarter than them—how come their church is going better than mine?" Or "They're smarter than me, but my evangelism is more effective than theirs!" Or perhaps we say, "Their church may have attracted more people, but only because they have sold out to xxx—we are much more theologically robust!" Or we think quietly to ourselves (for we are much too godly to say it aloud and make ourselves look bad), "She is a much better speaker than me—but I have much more depth" or "He is such a great evangelist, but you know what? I am a nicer person!" Comparison, it seems, is an occupational hazard—but only if you are a living, breathing member of the human race.

The problem is that every time we do it—every time we look at another person and measure ourselves against them—we are throwing the door wide open to pride (if we can find a way to score ourselves higher than them) or its twin sister, self-pity (if we can't). Every time we compare, we throw living by grace through faith out the window and start to run with

> Every time we compare ourselves with others, we swap living to please God with living to please ourselves, under the guise of impressing other people.

a gospel of good works. Every time we compare, we swap living to please God with living to please ourselves, under the guise of impressing other people—and it stinks! What undergirds this passage is Jesus' teaching in Matthew 7:

> "Judge not, that you be not judged. For with the judgment you pronounce you will be judged, and with the measure you use it will be measured to you. Why do you see the speck that is in your brother's eye, but do not notice the log that is in your own eye? Or how can you say to your brother, "Let me take the speck out of your eye," when there is the log in your own eye? You hypocrite, first take the log out of your own eye, and then you will see clearly to take the speck out of your brother's eye." (Matthew 7:2-7)

This is what kept Paul from bitterness and ensured that he stayed on track over the years—he didn't succumb to comparisons but focused on the work of the kingdom.

Is this an issue for you? As you read this now, I am confident that there will be more than a few of us who are ruining our own happiness in Christ by comparing ourselves with others. And in doing so, we are either slipping into an odious superiority or a self-indulgent self-pity—both of which are a slap in the face to the Christ who rescued us and treasures us, even in our self-regarding stupidity.

Which flows neatly into the next principle which enabled Paul to cope with and flourish despite no small amount of stress...

Habit 6: Focus on what God has given you to do

There is a delicious freedom in knowing what God has—and hasn't—given us to do—and sticking to it. That was something that Paul's opponents weren't so good at. It seems that they were extremely keen to take over—and take the credit from Paul. But Paul was very careful to keep things in perspective. You can see that in 2 Corinthians **10:13-15**:

> "But we will not boast beyond limits, but will boast only with regard to the area of influence God assigned to us ... we are not overextending ourselves ... We do not boast beyond limit in the labours of others."

Paul maintains that God gave him the responsibility to look after the new church at Corinth, and that he is determined to follow that through. That's why he can't just stand idly by and let these interlopers destabilise everything. In insisting on payment, and emphasising rhetoric over content, and over-valuing education, status and reputation, they are undermining the message of the gospel.

Paul isn't a control freak, but he does have a profound sense of pastoral responsibility. These church members in Corinth—no matter how annoying they may be—are a gift from God to him, and he isn't going to walk away completely. But nor is he going to get carried away, and start throwing his weight about in areas that are beyond his "jurisdiction". Paul is focused on what God has given him to do, which is to plant churches, establish churches, and see the church spread across the entire Mediterranean. And he won't be deflected from that.

Verses 15-17 spell out that even though Paul is very committed to the existing church, he is also committed to seeing the gospel spread across the region. He longs to see the faith of the Corinthians increase, so that "as our area of influence among you may be greatly enlarged", Corinth might prove to be a launching pad for future gospel ministry, "so that we may preach the gospel in lands beyond you". But Paul's method in this was strictly non-competitive. The last thing he wanted to do was to take credit for "work already done in another's area of influence". His overarching conviction is "Let the one who boasts, boast in the Lord". His opponents desperately wanted to steal some glory for themselves; Paul's only concern is to see the gospel spread and God's glory increase.

Paul's job was to plant churches and see the gospel reach as many Gentiles as possible. He says the same thing to the Romans in Romans 15:

"In Christ Jesus, then, I have reason to be proud of my work for God. For I will not venture to speak of anything except what Christ has accomplished through me to bring the Gentiles to obedience—by word and deed, by the power of signs and wonders, by the power of the Spirit of God—so that from Jerusalem and all the way around to Illyricum I have fulfilled the ministry of the gospel of Christ; and thus I make it my ambition to preach the gospel, not where Christ has already been named, lest I build on someone else's foundation, but as it is written, 'Those who have never been told of him will see, and those who have never heard will understand'." (Romans 15:17-21)

There are few places in the New Testament where the balance between focusing on the work of the local church and longing to see the gospel reach entire nations is so beautifully expressed. Paul knew that God himself had entrusted the church at Corinth to him, but he also knew that his mission was to play his part in bringing about the obedience of faith among the Gentiles—so he got on with it, safe in the knowledge that anything that advanced this mission would be, by definition a good thing. It is this which undergirds his gospel generosity to other co-workers and brothers on the one hand, and his readiness to face down unhelpful influences, home and away, on the other.

So we need to make sure that we focus on the specific local task that God has given us, while not forgetting that we are also called to play our part in the great-commission work of taking the gospel to the whole world. If we do that, we will be neither proprietorial nor short-sighted. Which takes us to the last component of a robust gospel ministry that will thrive even in the face of strong opposition.

Habit 7: Live to please God

It's hardly rocket science—Paul draws the chapter to a close with these simple words:

> "For it is not the one who commends himself who is approved,
> but the one whom the Lord commends." (2 Corinthians **10:18**)

I recently heard about a colleague who filled out the feedback form at a conference by giving 1/10 for every part of the programme in which he wasn't involved, and 10/10 to the sessions he spoke at, writing with his tongue firmly in his cheek, "_____'s sessions were peer-less—please have him back every year". The organisers quickly saw the joke and disregarded his feedback. That's because self-commendation is basically meaningless, and even more so in a Christian con-text—because the only approval that actually matters come from God.

Nowhere is that clearer than in Jesus' parable of the talents, where he holds out to us the glorious prospect of these words:

> "Well done, good and faithful servant. You have been faithful

over a little; I will set you over much. Enter into the joy of your
master." (Matthew 25:23)

This is to be our great goal That's why Paul tells us in 2 Timothy 2:15,
"Do your best to present yourself to God as one approved, a worker
who has no need to be ashamed, rightly handling the word of truth".
Ultimately, it is living like this—living to please the Lord Jesus—which
sets us free to cope with conflict and opposition, and criticism, and
slights, and to do it all with a deeply secure smile on our faces. That's
what Paul models for us, and that's what we are called to.

The key to living for Jesus

There is, in this chapter, a rich and delicate balance between being
gentle because of the gospel and demolishing unchristian strongholds through the gospel; between putting our confidence in Christ
alone and committing ourselves wholeheartedly to being consistent;
between focusing on the local church and trying to reach the world;
between not comparing ourselves to others and living to please God.
One question remains—how did Paul pull this off? Or better, *how can
we pull this off?* In particular, how on earth can we hope to maintain
this balance, this godly poise, when we're under pressure? How can
ordinary people like us hope to deal with patronising, hostile, dismiss-
ive opposition like this?

The answer is simple—Paul found it back in the Old Testament, and
he quotes it in 2 Corinthians **10:17**:

> "Thus says the LORD: 'Let not the wise man boast in his wisdom, let
> not the mighty man boast in his might, let not the rich man boast
> in his riches, but let him who boasts boast in this, that he under-
> stands and knows me, that I am the LORD who practices steadfast
> love, justice, and righteousness in the earth. For in these things I
> delight,' declares the LORD." (Jeremiah 9:23-24)

Let him who boasts, boast in the Lord! The key to living for Jesus is to
treasure him above all things. May God help us to do that, and may

it transform the way we think, and speak, and plan, and stand, and hurt, and respond.

Questions for reflection

1. Why is consistency such a big deal for followers of Jesus?

2. Who do you compare yourself with and why? What does this reveal about your heart?

3. What stands in the way of our living to please God?

10. HOW TO BE A COMPLETE IDIOT

2 Corinthians chapters 11 and 12 are among the most challenging in the New Testament. Paul's highly emotional appeal to this church with which he has such strong ties now takes a completely unexpected turn. In a last-gasp attempt to get the Corinthians to embrace gospel-shaped wisdom (rather than the Corinthian version which they were in danger of falling into), Paul explains how to be a complete idiot on the one hand and how to be wise on the other.

I think it's fair to say that this is a part of the Bible like no other. Paul writes this passage with tears in his eyes and his tongue firmly in his cheek. These chapters are dripping with irony and yet full of tender concern, as Paul takes the words of Proverbs to heart, and answers the foolish Corinthians according to their not inconsiderable folly. First, in 2 Corinthians 11:1-15, he deals with their idiocy in embracing the false teachers whom he tackled head on in the previous chapter. Then, in a remarkable passage which runs from 11:16 – 12:13, Paul paints the most vivid picture of true wisdom. So let's start with how to be a complete idiot in four simple steps!

Step 1: Ignore the people who love you most

Paul's long-running saga with the church at Corinth had, in recent times, been immeasurably complicated by the fact that they had bought into the message and style of the part-Christian, part-Jewish, part-Sophist journeymen philosophers who had come plying their half-baked teaching after Paul had left. The believers had ditched Paul and his message for these exploitative entrepreneurs. So Paul writes, "I wish you would bear with me in a little foolishness. Do bear with me!" **(11:1)**. We'll see why he says that in a moment. Then in **verse 2** Paul casts himself as the father of the bride, who has committed himself to getting his daughter to her wedding without her running off with someone else—and it is not going well. The Corinthians have been beguiled by a slick suitor, and Paul is desperately trying to talk some sense into them. Paul loves them, and God himself loves them—how could they possibly be wooed away by anyone else? If you want to be an idiot, then ignore those who love you the most. This picture is strikingly helpful: it has something profound to teach about discipleship and ministry.

> If you want to be an idiot, then ignore those who love you the most.

There is something in all of us which is drawn to people who make us feel good—who say nice things about us. But the stubborn and unfortunate truth is that people who say nice things about us all the time simply aren't telling the truth. Unfortunately, you are not that nice, and neither am I. And those who love us—those who really love us—will want to see us grow in the likeness of Jesus as we are transformed through the gospel in the power of the Spirit. And that means that sometimes they will say things to us that aren't particularly pleasant to hear. Do you have people who say that stuff to you? If you don't, ask God to bring them into your life. If you do, then thank God for them, and make sure you spend time with them talking about what really matters. Or, if you want to be an idiot, shut them out. If that's the discipleship lesson, what do we learn about ministry?

When it comes to ministry, we're not at the centre of the action. We're like the father of the bride; it will cost us a lot. And believe me, as the father of three girls, the fear I feel is real—both financially and emotionally. As you minister to people in whatever capacity, you are like the father of the bride at a wedding; you carry a heavy responsibility and you are deeply involved, but it is not ultimately about you! The twin goals of ministry are the glory of Christ and the joy of his church.

That means we need to be warmhearted and passionate, while remembering that it isn't actually about us at the end of the day. So, as Calvin warns, every Christian needs to...

> "beware of pursuing their own interests rather than Christ's, and of intruding themselves in his place, lest while they pretend to be the bridegroom's friends they are in fact adulterers who seduce the bride's love to themselves."
>
> (*Commentary on 2 Corinthians*, p 140)

Ministry matters, but it isn't about us. But if you want to be an idiot, then make it about you, and ignoring the people who love you the most will help enormously.

Step 2: Swap the truth for lies at every opportunity

Or, to put it more bluntly, *be gullible*! Paul had invested enormous amounts of energy and time, and had lavished love on this church—so it's no surprise that he was gutted when they so quickly lost their grip on everything he had taught them, swapping the gospel for lies.

According to **11:3-4**, they had embraced a different Jesus, a different Spirit and a different gospel. Just as "the serpent deceived Eve by his cunning", they had been misled from following Christ wholeheartedly. What had gone wrong? All it took was someone proclaiming "another Jesus" or offering "a different spirit" or even preaching "a different gospel", and they were off. Or, as Paul says, "You put up with it readily enough". This reflected pretty badly on the Corinthians, but what it said about their favourite teachers is even worse. The Corinthians were fools—but the philosophers were satanic.

Now you could be forgiven for thinking that's just a little bit over the top. There has been nothing so far to suggest that the teachers plaguing the church in Corinth were as bad as, say, those Judaisers who had shown up in Galatia (see, for example, Galatians 5:7-12) They were troublemakers, certainly. A bit bombastic and pompous, granted. But doing the work of the evil one? And yet that is precisely what Paul says. In the same way that the serpent gently suckered Eve into thinking that she and Adam could get away with less than wholehearted obedience (see Genesis 3:1-5), these teachers had encouraged the Corinthians down a similarly self-indulgent track. And because of that, Paul designates them as "enemies of the gospel". They—and the Corinthians—had swapped the truth for a lie. And that is always the way of the fool.

There is an old German proverb which says, "Tell me who you are fighting, and I'll tell you who you are". We'd do well to remember that. For while the last thing we want to be is a generation of people who devote ourselves to picking as many fights as we can in the years ahead, I suspect it is far more likely that the weakness of the church in the years to come will be that we aren't prepared to fight at all. When the truth is at stake, Paul is deeply intolerant. He is theologically far-sighted and realises that even though these teachers are basically **orthodox**, their practice, and in particular their arrogant rejection of the way of the cross, will, sooner or later, seep into the theological "water supply" of the church and poison it from within. So let me challenge you right now to set yourself to hold onto the truth, and to ask God to give you a highly sensitive theological radar for the sake of the church in the years to come. Be ready to think through the implications of every new idea, and be ready to fight for the truth. Unless you want to be a complete idiot, don't swap the truth for lies.

Step 3: Be impressed by show

We don't know if Paul coined the term "super-apostles" or if they themselves did. Either way, I think we can guess how Paul felt about their claims, and the fact that they had sucked the Corinthians in: "I consider that I am not in the least inferior to these super-apostles" (2 Corinthians **11:5**). It was fairly pathetic really. The church at Corinth had extended exposure to the greatest church-planter/theologian the world has ever seen, and they didn't rate him. They should have seen plainly from his visits that he was the real deal. They should have seen clearly from Paul's first letter to Corinth—which they had received a year or so before—the kind of man they were dealing with. But no. The Corinthians preferred these "super-apostles".

I once heard a story about a group of tourists bumping into an old guy while hiking in the foothills of the Himalayas. They asked him to take their photo in front of Mount Everest, and sent him on his way. Only later did it dawn on them that the old guy was Sir Edmund Hillary—one of the first men to climb Everest. I do wonder if the Corinthians were ever embarrassed by their failure to be impressed by Paul. Look at what Paul has to write to them in **verse 6**:

"Even if I am unskilled in speaking [literally: 'an idiot'], I am not so
  in knowledge; indeed, in every way we have made this plain to
  you in all things."

Bruce Winter has suggested that to be an *"idiotes"* is to be trained in rhetoric, but not to make use of its techniques (Bruce Winter, *Philo and Paul Among the Sophists*, p 224-25). And that may be the point here. Paul refuses to indulge in the showboating that marked the travelling philosophy circus. But whether that's right or not, the believers should have realised that when it came to knowing God and the gospel, Paul was the real deal. The problem is that the real deal isn't actually what we are looking for. We are all too impressed by show.

Discernment is a much underrated gift. Even when it comes to the church, it seems that there is one born every minute. We are all susceptible to being sucked in. I think it's partly because of our own insecurity. Most of us feel our weaknesses so acutely that when someone shows up who is strong where we think we are weak, we tend to be oblivious to their own weaknesses, obvious though they may be. This was an inherent weakness in the church in Corinth (see 1 Corinthians 1:26-29). Their background left them vulnerable to being far too easily impressed by show.

And that's actually the way it is for all of us. We tend to be impressed by people who touch the raw nerve of our own vulnerabilities. So just to check—have you thought about that? Who gets past your defences, because they are just a little bit like the person you wish you were? It's worth thinking about—unless, of course, you want to be an idiot. In which case you should ignore the people who love you, give up on the truth, be impressed by show, and fourth, respect those who exploit you!

Step 4: Respect those who exploit you

By this stage, I hope you can pick up a sense of Paul's frustration and bewilderment at the behaviour of the church at Corinth. He really had done his level best to win them over for Christ and the gospel. But even his best efforts seemed to rebound. In particular, the fact that he was adamant that he wasn't going to charge for preaching had backfired.

Paul knew very well that in Corinth, as in much of the Graeco-Roman world, speakers got paid to speak and audiences paid to listen to them. The assumption was that you got what you paid for, and on the principle that there's no such thing as a free lunch, speakers who didn't charge weren't worth listening to. But for Paul, that the gospel of grace comes to us freely was *so important* that he was willing to go against those cultural norms—and the assumption that manual labour was demeaning—for the sake of his message. But you can see the result in 2 Corinthians **11:7**, where he actually has to defend himself by asking if he had sinned by "humbling myself so that you might be exalted, because I preached God's gospel to you free of charge?" The Corinthians were so mixed up that even though God exalts people all the way through the Bible for doing what Paul did (humbling himself), they labelled it a sin.

Paul had humbled himself on every visit (see 1 Corinthians 9:12; 2 Corinthians **11:8**). He didn't even ask for support for himself or take on a local benefactor (**v 9**). He used Macedonian money to live off, so he says he "refrained and will refrain from burdening you in any way". The problem is that the Corinthians didn't recognise self-sacrifice and humility when they saw it! Instead they despised Paul, and honoured the hucksters who were messing with their heads!

Paul understood that one of the easiest ways to discredit the gospel is by making accusations of "being in it for the money". Ambrosiaster, a fourth-century writer, explains:

> "Paul refused payment for two reasons. He would not resemble the false apostles who were preaching for their own advantage and not for the glory of God, nor would he allow the vigour of his message to become sluggish. For the person who accepts payment from sinners loses the authority to censure them."
>
> (Commentary on Paul's Epistles)

This approach was fundamental to Paul's mission in the whole region, and he wasn't about to be deflected (**v 10**). He insists that it's crazy to say *Paul doesn't love us because he doesn't rip us off* (**v 11**). It was sheer madness to despise Paul, and respect the interlopers, who despite their claims, operated on a whole different set of principles. In an attempt to get them to face reality, Paul says, in **verse 12**, that he will keep doing what he is doing until they realise the difference between his methods and those of the people he describes in

> One of the easiest ways to discredit the gospel is by making accusations of "being in it for the money".

verse 13 as "false apostles, deceitful workmen, disguising themselves as apostles of Christ". He even goes so far as to identify them as servants of Satan (**v 14-15**), disguised as "servants of righteousness", who will be punished for their actions in due time. If you want to be an idiot, he suggests, then go ahead: respect the very people who are exploiting you.

It would be easy simply to despise the stupid Corinthians at this point. But let's remember, it is always much, much easier to spot other people's blind spots than our own. And then there is the fact that Satan is not stupid. Charles Hodge sagely pointed out in the nineteenth century that…

> "Satan doesn't come to us as Satan, neither does sin present itself to us as sin."
>
> (*I & II Corinthians,* p 641)

It is easy to be fooled. Being an idiot takes remarkably little effort, as the Corinthians proved with some panache. Getting it wrong comes naturally to most of us. So what can we do?

With God's help, we can listen to those who love us, and hold onto the truth, and be impressed by the real deal, and respect those who teach us the gospel and model it. We can be *wise,* which is exactly where Paul takes us in part two of this passage.

Questions for reflection

1. One of the first steps to growing in godliness is facing the fact that we are *not* naturally wise, and so we need God's help to live well. Have you embraced your own inner idiot?

2. Why do we often push away the people who love us most?

3. Why are we so susceptible to swapping the truth of the gospel for lies? What can we do to guard against that?

PART TWO

How to be wise

What comes next is just about the most surprising, if not the most confusing passage in all of Paul's letters—because Paul boasts. He clearly isn't comfortable doing it, but it's equally clear he feels that he has no option. Matthew Henry helpfully said:

"As much against the grain as it is for a proud man to acknowledge his infirmities, so much is it against the grain for a humble
man to speak in his own praise."

*(An Exposition of the Several Epistles
Contained in the New Testament,* p 152)

Which goes some way to explaining the awkwardness throughout this section. Paul starts in **11:16** by saying,

"I repeat, let no one [and specifically, none of the false teachers]
think me foolish. But even if you do [think I'm a fool], accept me
as a fool, so that I too may boast a little."

Indulge me for a minute, he says. *As you are so into boasting, let me boast for a moment.* Paul says, *I know I'm being an idiot, but stick with me.* The translation of **verse 17** is tricky, but Paul explains: "What I am saying with [literally 'my boasting strategy'] I say not with the Lord's authority, but as a fool". Paul says, in effect, *I don't like doing this—it's not godly; but I'm going to anyway.* Why does he do it? Because the Corinthians are so into boasting in achievements (**verse 18**). Because they listen to fools who are false teachers rambling on, so they can listen to him for a bit (**verse 19**). Because they are so foolish, **verse 20**, that "if someone makes slaves of you, or devours you, or takes advantage of you, or puts on airs, or strikes you in the face", then they stick with him. If they can do that, then perhaps listening to Paul run with the "fool" thing for just a minute might help them to snap out of it. In a statement dripping with irony, Paul even says in **verse 21** that "To my shame, I must say, we were too weak for that": that is, too weak to exploit you—*But I can parody the false teachers in an effort to get you to see sense.*

Now this is clearly a high-risk strategy; Calvin says:

"Such dwelling on our excellence is always dangerous, for like a man entering a labyrinth, we are soon hemmed in by it, and become too aware of our gifts and too ignorant of ourselves."

(*Commentary on 2 Corinthians*, p 155)

But for Paul, this really is the last roll of the dice. He has nothing left in reserve—it's all or nothing, as he makes a last desperate bid to get through to the Corinthians for the sake of the gospel. And with that, the stage is set. So what does he say?

1. Boast in your sufferings, not your successes

If you must boast, Paul says, boast not in your successes but in your suffering. For some reason, the false teachers were boasting of their impeccable Jewish heritage. But Paul could easily match them in that. If they play the foolish "Whose resumé is more impressive?" game (**v 21**), then Paul wins hands down. In **verses 22-23**, he reminds the Corinthians of his impeccable qualifications: "Are they Hebrews? So am I. Are they Israelites? So am I. Are they offspring of Abraham? So am I. Are they servants of Christ? I am a better one."

> If you must boast, Paul says, boast not in your successes but in your suffering.

Now at this point, one might expect Paul's resumé to run something like this: *I have preached in more places, I have written more books, I have planted more churches, I have revitalised more churches, I have established more multi-site churches, I have spoken at bigger events, I have got more letters after my name…* But Paul isn't going there—not for one second. If he is going to carry out this mad boasting strategy, he is going to boast about…

"… far greater labours, far more imprisonments, with countless beatings, and often near death." (**v 23**)

When he comes to **verse 24**, he even starts detailing his punishments: "Five times I received at the hands of the Jews the forty lashes less one". Deuteronomy 25:3 limited the beating anyone got to 40—by Paul's day they had reduced it to a mere 39, which was 13 strokes of a triple-stranded whip—first on the front, and then on the back.

Then there was Roman punishment. Roman citizens were exempt, but that didn't stop Paul being beaten with a rod three times (2 Corinthians **11:25**). Oh, and he was also stoned, as well as being shipwrecked three times (which doesn't count Acts 27, which took place after this was written); including being left adrift at sea for 24 hours. And that's not to mention regular scary experiences on the dangerous roads of the first century and crossing rivers, plus "danger from robbers, danger from my own people, danger from Gentiles, danger in the city, danger in the wilderness, danger at sea, danger from false brothers" ((2 Corinthians **11:26**). One gets the feeling that he really wants the Corinthians to get this point, so he goes on and on.

In **verse 27**, he lists hard work, sleepless nights, going hungry and thirsty regularly, and being cold. And then there was the spiritual and emotional toil of "the daily pressure on me of my anxiety for all the churches" (**v 28**). He reminds them that he lives the experience of all the churches he has visited and knows about blow by blow: "Who is weak, and I am not weak? Who is made to fall, and I am not indignant?" (**v 29**). The hammer blow comes in **verse 30**—this is the life of an authentic apostle, so he says, "if I must boast, I will boast of the things that show my weakness". He backs this up in the strongest terms with an appeal to God as his witness (**v 31**).

Not long before Paul wrote these words, Augustus Caesar had decided to celebrate his own achievements by ensuring that his self-penned funerary inscription, *res gestae divi Augusti* (the deeds of the divine Augustus), would be engraved on all manner of statues and public buildings throughout the Roman Empire. Augustus had no problem with boasting in his greatness; the inscription has 35 very specific paragraphs on why "I love me." This would have been part of

> It is when you really can't cope that God is seen to be the great Provider.

the cultural wallpaper when Paul was growing up as a young Roman citizen. Paul's version is a bit different because it boasts about his suffering for Christ, both physically and emotionally, in the beatings he received and the compassion he feels for the churches he has planted. So do you want to be wise? Then boast in your sufferings: realise that it is when you really can't cope, when you are struggling, that God is seen to be the great provider.

2. Boast in your disgrace

After this, Paul moves on to what was not exactly his finest hour. But he boasts of this too. After invoking God himself in the strongest possible terms as his witness ("The God and Father of the Lord Jesus, he who is blessed for ever, knows that I am not lying") in **11:31**, in **verses 32-33**, he reminds his readers of the day when he was forced to flee from Damascus because "the governor under King Aretas was guarding the city of Damascus in order to seize me". His departure was ignominious to say the least: "I was let down in a basket through a window in the wall and escaped his hands".

The *corona muralis* (walled crown) was the ancient equivalent of the Victoria Cross or the Medal of Honor. This highest of honours was given to the first guy to scale the wall when attacking a city. But Paul doesn't boast about being first up the wall, but being first down it. Don Carson says, "the man who had access to the highest officials in Jerusalem slunk out of Damascus like a criminal, lowered like a catch of dead fish in a basket whose smelly cargo he'd displaced." (*From Triumphalism to Maturity*, p 128) Paul doesn't explain why King Aretas was so cranky with him—but it probably had something to do with upsetting him during the ten unrecorded years he spent in Syria and Arabia before his first missionary journey. But whatever the reason, his departure from Damascus was a real low point in his life—and yet Paul insists on boasting about it. And he isn't finished yet. For in chapter 12, he goes on to *boast in his weakness*.

3. Boast in your weakness

This is one of the most unusual passages in the whole of the New Testament, but having traced Paul's argument (and his boasting experiment) through chapter 11, his point is relatively clear. Paul begins by reminding us that he is still in boasting mode, even though "there is nothing to be gained by it" (for normal, well-adjusted people). But for the sake of the Corinthians, he will stick with it in the hope of getting through to them. In particular, he says, in **12:1**, that "I will go on to visions and revelations of the Lord".

Now at this stage, Paul's argument takes another unexpected turn, as he switches to the third person in **verse 2**: "I know a man in Christ who fourteen years ago was caught up to the third heaven"—probably referring to God's throne room in the heavenly holy of holies. Paul doesn't tell us explicitly who this is or even what actually happened: "Whether in the body or out of the body I do not know, God knows. And I know that this man was caught up into paradise—whether in the body or out of the body I do not know, God knows" (v 2-3)— and to cap it all, Paul won't even tell us anything that was seen or reported—"and he heard things that cannot be told, which man may not utter" (**v 4**).

Down the years three options have been proposed for the identity of this person—(i) one of Paul's friends; (ii) a **parody** of the super-apostles; or (iii) Paul himself, which is the most plausible solution. His discomfort with talking about himself has already been clear; now, because he is talking about a privileged experience, he is doubly sensitive, and *because the vision isn't actually the point*, he switches to the third person to deflect attention from it, and get to his actual point, which comes in verse 5.

Yes, he did have a unique vision of God in his throne room at the heart of the heavenly Eden. You can see that from **verses 5-6**:

"On behalf of this man I will boast, but on my own behalf I will not boast, except of my weaknesses. Though if I should wish to boast, I would not be a fool, for I would be speaking the truth. [But he's not going to go there] I refrain from it, so that no one may think more of me than he sees in me or hears from me."

In passing, Paul makes the point that if anyone is going to judge him, or anyone else for that matter, they should do it on the basis of what they see or hear, not on what experiences such a person may or may not have had. Paul's own experience could match—or even outstrip—anything the super-apostles could lay claim to. But for Paul, the advantage that flowed from this great privilege was that it led to a deeper experience of weakness.

The reason Paul has reluctantly shared any of this becomes clear in **verse 7**: as a result of this startling vision, God gave him "a thorn … in the flesh, a messenger of Satan to harass me", in order to stop him from becoming big-headed. Paul was not keen on this experience—and actually asked God explicitly three times to take it away, but to no avail (**v 8**). Again, Paul holds back the details; he doesn't tell us whether this was mental illness, bad eyesight, a poor marriage, or something completely different, like the opposition he routinely faces around the Mediterranean—because that's not the point. The point is that God acted (by giving Satan permission) to torment him—*why*? So that Paul would hear God say, "My grace is sufficient for you, for my power is made perfect in weakness", and so that Paul himself would learn to live out the principle of **verses 9-10**:

"Therefore I will boast all the more gladly of my weaknesses, so that the power of Christ may rest upon me. For the sake of Christ, then, I am content with weaknesses, insults, hardships, persecutions, and calamities. For when I am weak, then I am strong."

This takes us right to the heart of what it means to be a Christian. This is real wisdom—to boast in our sufferings, in our disgrace, in our weakness. This is the wisdom of the cross. This is where we find grace. This is where we find strength. This is why, for Paul, there is so much riding on this that it is worth playing the fool in these chapters, in order that these people, whom he loves so deeply, will rediscover the wisdom of God—the wisdom of which he wrote back at the start of his first letter (see 1 Corinthians 1:20-31).

> This is real wisdom—to boast in our sufferings, in our disgrace, in our weakness.

Paul plays the fool to call them and us to find real wisdom at the foot of the cross. Real wisdom which says:

I will not boast of anything—no gifts, no power, no wisdom,
But I will boast in Jesus Christ, his death and resurrection.
> (Stuart Townend, "How deep the Father's Love for us")

In a way, this isn't all that complex. But it is profound. What are we boasting in? Is it the cross and resurrection of the Lord Jesus? Does he loom huge in our affections? In our ambitions? In our self-understanding? Is it about him or about us? If it's about us, it will show both in what we boast about and in whom we trust.

The end of the experiment

And with that, Paul's experiment with boasting comes to an end. Listen to how he finishes off this section in 2 Corinthians **12:11-13**:

"I have been a fool! You forced me to it, for I ought to have been commended by you. For I was not at all inferior to these super-apostles, even though I am nothing. The signs of a true apostle were performed among you with utmost patience, with signs and wonders and mighty works [pointing to the truth of Christ, making them gasp at Christ and encouraging them to bow before Christ]. For in what were you less favoured than the rest of the churches, except that I myself did not burden you? Forgive me this wrong!"

This brings his appeal to a close.

So what are we to do with all this? We may need to repent of being idiots—of looking at our world as if Christ had not died in our place, of being sucked in by people who are impressive but not godly. We may need to ask God for the wisdom and strength in weakness to live a life which is shaped in every part by the cross of Christ. Whatever it is, let's do it!

Questions for reflection

1. These chapters are deeply countercultural. How does your understanding of suffering differ from Paul's? Why do you think that is?

2. We are generally very keen to preserve and enhance our reputation. How does the gospel cut across that?

3. Why is it so hard to embrace (let alone boast about) our weakness? What will bring us to the point that Paul reaches at the end of 2 Corinthians 12?

11. LOVE WINS AGAIN

Richard Baxter, in his book *The Reformed* (that is, transformed) *Pastor,* written in 1656, says this about the importance of the *way* in which Christian workers serve Christ:

"The whole of our ministry must be carried on in tender love to our people. We must let them see that nothing pleases us but what profits them; and that what does them good does us good; and that nothing troubles us more than their hurt. We must feel toward our people, as a father toward his children: yea, the tenderest love of a mother must not surpass ours. We must even travail in birth, till Christ be formed in them … We ourselves will take all things well from one that we know doth entirely love us. We will put up with a blow that is given us in love, sooner than with a foul word that is spoken to us in malice or in anger. Most men judge counsel, as they judge the affection of him that gives it: at least, so far as to give it a fair hearing. Oh, therefore, see that you feel a tender love to your people in your breasts, and let them perceive it in your speeches, and see it in your conduct. Let them see that you spend, and are spent, for their sakes; and that all you do is for them, and not for any private ends of your own."

(*The Reformed Pastor,* p 59)

That's what it means to do ministry. In fact, this is what it means to be a follower of the Lord Jesus. And it takes us right to the heart of what this final section of 2 Corinthians is about. These final chapters are about love. The glorious news is that Jesus Christ himself both makes it possible for people like us to love like him and shows us what that love looks like in practice, and he does it all through his death and resurrection.

We are almost at the end of our journey through 2 Corinthians, which is surely Paul's warmest, most passionate, most vulnerable letter. It began with Paul walking his readers through his long relationship with them—four letters and a couple of visits—pleading with them and urging them to side with Jesus and the gospel, and with him (chapters 1 – 7). After getting an up-to-date report from Titus, he then calls the church family to come good on their commitment to help their struggling brothers and sisters in Jerusalem, by sending them money (chapters 8 – 9). He then takes on the false teachers who have been undermining his relationship with the Corinthians in chapter 10, and calls the church to be wise and to side with Christ in chapters 11 – 12. And now we come to the final section where this letter finishes, not with Paul on the defensive but very much on the front foot.

Paul assures them of his love for them one last time, as he calls them to press on for the sake of the gospel. So what can we expect from the conclusion to this letter? We can expect God to gather together all that he has been saying to us, as he presents us with what it means to love people as Paul did, as he followed Christ. We're going to walk through this passage in seven steps as we see Paul's Christ-like love in action.

1. Love pursues

Paul's first visit to Corinth had seen the church planted. His second hadn't been quite so special—Paul calls it "the sorrowful visit"—but he *didn't give up*—he would come a third time (**12:14**). Why? "For I seek not what is yours *but you*". As we have seen before, he is their spiritual father—he is the one who brought the gospel to Corinth—and he hasn't forgotten about them or moved on from them. In fact, he is taking his spiritual parental responsibilities very seriously indeed! Rather than sponging off them as a benefactor, he is their patron: "For children are not bound to save up for their parents, but parents for their children". Paul is committed to them and will not let them go, for love always pursues its object. And look at how that works out with Paul, "I will most gladly spend and be spent for your souls" (**v 15**).

Let that sink in… Paul is *utterly committed* to these half-hearted, confused believers—who, let's remember, had no doubt hurt him deeply by believing all kinds of lies and slander about him. But he is still so committed to them that he will not stop pursuing them—and, in fact, he says that he will "most gladly spend and be spent" for

> Paul is utterly committed to these half-hearted, confused believers. He will pour himself out for them.

their souls. He will *pour himself* out for them. The irony is, of course, that according to verse 15, they were so mixed up that as his love for them increased, theirs for him seemed to decrease—but not even that deters Paul. He still pursues the Corinthians because he loves them.

So what produces this kind of love for people? This willingness to stick with them, put up with them and pursue them at such real personal cost? Only one thing can do that in a human being, and that is the discovery that we have first been pursued by another. Paul had experienced that personally, when the same Jesus Christ whom he hated and whose followers he had hounded calmly caught up with him on the road to Damascus. And the end of one pursuit gave rise to the beginning of another, as Paul set out to be all things to all men in order that he might save some.

In the late 1890s, Francis Thompson wrote a 182-line poem which described his pursuit by God under the title *The Hound of Heaven*—and here's how it begins:

"I fled Him, down the nights and down the days;
  I fled Him, down the arches of the years;

> I fled Him, down the labyrinthine ways
>> Of my own mind; and in the mist of tears
> I hid from Him …
>> From those strong Feet that followed, followed after.
>>> But with unhurrying chase,
>>> And unperturbèd pace,
>> Deliberate speed, majestic instancy,
>>> They beat—and a Voice beat
>>> More instant than the Feet—
>> 'All things betray thee, who betrayest Me.' "

With unhurried yet breakneck speed, Christ has sought us, and wooed us, and won us, and shepherded us—so in the same way that he has given himself for us, we must lovingly pursue others. God does not give up on us. Who are you tempted to give up on? Who would you honestly like to run away from? Perhaps we all simply need to face the fact that love pursues.

2. Love gives

We've seen over and over again as we've worked through 2 Corinthians that Paul went to great lengths to ensure that the Corinthians couldn't mix him up with the philosophers working the religious circuit for cash. It was so important to Paul that the free offer of the gospel is backed up by the fact that we are always giving, not taking—that's the way of love.

The ironic thing was that Paul had a hard time from the Corinthians over this. They accused him of some kind of double bluff—feigning generosity while somehow being on the make. You can see the accusation reflected in **verse 16**. And Paul's response? Paul's reply is actually very straightforward; he points to his record and that of the rest of his inner circle. They had consistently acted with integrity and generosity, and even more than that, they constantly put themselves out for the sake of the Corinthians. None of his emissaries exploited them. The most recent envoy, Titus, certainly didn't (**v 17-18**). That's because *real, God-given love* doesn't take, it gives.

To be a Christian is to adopt a stance which makes us ready to give at a moment's notice. *Why?* Because as the apostle John says so powerfully in 1 John 4:11, "Beloved, if God so loved us, we also ought to love one another". The "so loved us" bit, is of course, the engine which drives gospel-shaped love. Here's how John defines it in the preceding verses:

"Beloved, let us love one another, for love is from God, and whoever loves has been born of God and knows God. Anyone who
does not love does not know God, because God is love. In this
the love of God was made manifest among us, that God sent his
only Son into the world, so that we might live through him. In
this is love, not that we have loved God but that he loved us and
sent his Son to be the **propitiation** for our sins." (1 John 4:7-10)

Love gives because God has given supremely in the death of the Lord Jesus Christ. Have you got this? Because this is the mark of authentic Christianity.

Here is Richard Baxter again:

"To this end the works of charity are necessary, as far as your estate
will reach; for bare words will hardly convince men that you have
any great love to them. But, if you are not able to give, show that
you are willing to give if you had it, and do that sort of good you
can. But see that your love be not *carnal*, flowing from pride, as
one that is a suitor for himself rather than for Christ, and, therefore, doth love because he is loved, or that he may be loved."

(*The Reformed Pastor,* p 59)

3. Love builds

Just in case the Corinthians have missed his point up to now, Paul spells it out for them in 2 Corinthians **12:19**. Rather than defend-ing himself, he simply states that "in the sight of God … we have been speaking in Christ, and all for your upbuilding, beloved". If you want a statement that sums up everything we have seen in this letter about serving Christ by serving one another, his church, then this is it—speaking in Christ to build other people up in the sight of God. Real ministry is always accountable to God, saturated in and motivated by Christ himself, and has the clear aim of building up the church. Everything Paul did was done with the clear purpose of building up the Corinthians.

For Paul, and every other New Testament writer, the twin purposes of the church are to reach out in evangelism and to strengthen one another in **edification**. We grow out and grow up to the glory of God. The love of Christ pursues and gives so that it *may build*. This is your role and mine—and it will be for the rest of our lives.

> God is building his church, and it is our responsibility, and our great privilege, to fall into line with that agenda.

Our involvement with the people of God locally—and across our city, our nation and our world—must be controlled by this simple fact: *God is building his church*, and it is our responsibility, and our great privilege, to fall into line with that agenda. And if we get this, if it is burned into our souls, then we will spend the rest of our lives pouring our hearts and souls into seeing the people of God built up. We won't always be thanked for it. It may sometimes feel to people that "being built up" seems awfully like being ripped apart. George Guthrie comments that "being built up sometimes feels like being torn down, especially when the edification comes wrapped in confrontation and correction" (*Second Corinthians,* p 618). But this is what love does.

And because it is the very nature of love to build, that will set our agenda and shape our desires for the local church. It will create in us a holy discontent with the status quo that God will use for the benefit of his people and his mission in this world. Because love builds, that dictates what we will look for and long for in the local church, and if it is missing, it will grieve us to the very core.

For if there is no desire for and plan for evangelism, we are short on love. If there is no thought of new initiatives (church plants, revitalisations and gospel partnerships between churches, for example), we are short on love. If there is no concern to see the gospel penetrate the hardest places, we are short on love. If there is no desire to send people to take the message of Christ to the nations, we are short on love. If there is no desire to see people become more like Christ, we are short on love. If there is no desire to see people grow in their love and knowledge of Christ, we are short on love. If there is no concern that people should be gripped and transformed by the glory of Christ, we are short on love.

This all flows from the simple fact that love builds.

Questions for reflection

1. Love can never be content to let relationships with brothers and sisters die—why would any of us do that? Is there a relationship you need to ask God for the grace to lovingly pursue right now?

2. All of us are more than capable of being selfish in relationships. Why is that so wrong if we belong to Jesus?

3. If love builds, what is our primary responsibility to one another? How do you think we might carry this out?

PART TWO

The final movement of Paul's second (published) letter to the church at Corinth is a declaration of Paul's Christ-like love for the church that he had planted. We have already seen how this love pursues, gives and builds. Now we also see that real love *mourns*.

4. Love mourns

It's hard to miss the fact that Paul is genuinely anxious about the future of his relationship with the Corinthians. The flip side of his longing to see them built up is a deep sadness—he even calls it "mourning" over them when they appear to be drifting away—because love mourns.

Paul has deferred this visit for as long as possible. He's worried that there may be "quarrelling, jealousy, anger, hostility, slander, gossip, conceit, and disorder". After all, his last visit revealed that someone was sleeping with his mother-in-law, and that person had to be **excommunicated** (see 1 Corinthians 5:1-5); these fears are real! In 2 Corinthians **12: 21**, Paul ramps it up still further. His great worry is that "God may humble me before you" as he has to come to terms with an even greater mess in the church. In other words, he is scared that things have got worse rather than better, "and I may have to mourn over many of those who sinned earlier and have not repented of the impurity, sexual immorality, and sensuality that they have practised".

Paul's concern is that when he shows up, all his past efforts—writing 1 Corinthians included—won't actually have solved anything, and he will have to face the fact that he has done an ineffective job in trying to help the church in Corinth get back on track; and he knows that this will be heartbreaking. He is scared that there will be relational disappointment, or dysfunctional relationships, or sexual immorality, or a combination of all three. *Why is he scared about this?* Because he cares.

This, for me, has been one of the standout features of this letter. Paul cares desperately for the Corinthians, even though they have been the bane of his life. So he rejoices when they are on track, and he grieves when they have lost the plot. And this, for me, has been the single great challenge of this letter: to make sure, whatever else I do, whatever else happens, that I pour myself into loving people with a love that pursues, gives, builds and mourns.

So how do we do this? How do we love people following Paul as he follows Jesus? First, let me say it has nothing to do with your personality type—whether you are an **INTJ** or an **ESFP**, a reformer or a peacemaker, a hugger or a non-hugger, you have the responsibility to love people "earnestly from a pure heart", to quote 1 Peter 1:22.

So how do we do that? The key is simple—we need to die to ourselves, meaning that we need to be more concerned about others than we are about ourselves. It's not complicated; it's just hard, especially when you are inveterately selfish. Whether you were brought up to think that you are the centre of the universe or you have had a fairly painful life, and have had to bunker down and protect yourself and survive, neither helps much. But the gentle work of the gospel in our

> We need to die to ourselves, meaning that we need to be more concerned about others than we are about ourselves.

lives assures us of the love and safety and affirmation and acceptance that we have in Christ through faith and repentance. This assurance enables us to gradually stop fretting about ourselves, thinking about ourselves and talking about ourselves. Those gospel assurances are the oxygen we need to breathe freely, and to start to see beyond ourselves, to think beyond ourselves, to ask questions and to listen to answers, and to love and to care, with a rich mixture of joy and mourning. This is the depth of love for his people which Christ produces in us.

5. Love confronts

At the start of 2 Corinthians 13, Paul paves the way for his third visit to Corinth (**v 1**). There is a lot of discussion as to why Paul quotes Deuteronomy 19:15 here, but in all probability it explains itself—Paul is saying, in effect, that his first two visits were like two eyewitness reports. This next visit would satisfy the burden of proof needed to ascertain if there was a real and ongoing problem in the church. If that proves to be the case, the problem needs to be confronted head on. And Paul is *very* clear that if there is blatant sin in the church, he will name it and shame it: "I warn them now while absent, as I did when present on my second visit, that if I come again I will not spare them" (2 Corinthians **13:2**). This is part and parcel of how Christ works powerfully in his church through his word. Paul states this baldly in **verse 3**: "He is not weak in dealing with you but is powerful among you".

Paul then returns to the idea of Christ working through our weakness in **verse 4**: "For he was crucified in weakness but lives by the power of God. For we also are weak in him, but in dealing with you we will live with him by the power of God." The logic runs like this:

- Christ embraced our weakness, dying in our place on the cross,

- but he is no longer weak, living by the power of God.

- In Christ then, even though I as his apostle am weak,

- as I explain his word, Christ himself will act in the power of God.

Paul's weakness doesn't stop him from acting to confront sin and ungodliness in the strength which Christ supplies, which is mediated through his word.

I suspect that often we hide behind *humility* to allow ourselves to avoid hard conversations. If I may say it respectfully, 2 Corinthians 13:1-4 blows that argument out of the water. Rather than hindering this pursuing, giving, edifying, mourning, confronting love, our weakness is the key to it, as it ensures that we don't mix up what we can and should do (speak the truth in love) with what Christ himself does: dealing powerfully among us through his word.

Listen to Richard Baxter once more:

"Take heed, therefore, that you do not connive at the sins of your people, under pretence of love, for that were to cross the nature and end of love. Friendship must be cemented by piety. A wicked man cannot be a true friend; and, if you befriend their wickedness, you show that you are wicked yourselves. Pretend not to love them, if you favour their sins, and seek not their salvation. By favouring their sins, you will show your enmity to God; and then how can you love your brother? If you be their best friends, help them against their worst enemies. And think not all sharpness inconsistent with love: parents correct their children, and God himself 'chastens every son whom he receives'."

(*The Reformed Pastor,* p 59)

Augustine says it a bit more succinctly: "Better it is to love even with the accompaniment of severity, than to mislead by (excess of) lenience".

I think this is one of the great cultural challenges we face in many places today. We really don't do confronting. And when we do it, we don't do it very well. We are too private, too independent, too proud, perhaps even too selfish. But holding one another at arm's length, and silently insisting on our autonomy flies in the face of the radical one-anotherness of the New Testament, and, in the light of this passage, undermines the confronting love which God calls us to in Christ.

6. Love challenges

As well as confronting what is very clearly and obviously wrong, love constantly pushes God's people to make sure that they keep going and keep growing, which is clear from **verses 5-6**: "Examine yourselves, to see whether you are in the faith". Paul backs that up with a further instruction: "Test yourselves. Or do you not realise this about yourselves, that Jesus Christ is in you?—unless indeed you fail to meet the test! I hope you will find out that we have not failed the test." The false teachers have caused a huge amount of confusion—confusion over Paul's orthodoxy, confusion over the truth of the gospel and clearly also confusion about the Corinthians' own salvation. So Paul encourages them to examine themselves to see whether they are "in the faith". He does this multiple times in Romans and in Colossians and here.

Since the **Reformation**, Bible Christians have usually shied away from this kind of language. We don't want people to turn inwards but outward to the objective work of Christ on our behalf. But Paul has no problem in using this language—*why?* Because he wants his readers to take hold of the obvious—that Christ has brought them to repentance and faith, and that these markers are signs of new life—that "Jesus Christ is in you" (2 Corinthians **13:5**). Or he wants them to face the fact that they are not yet believers (that they have failed the test). This is the loving thing to do—to gently push people to the assurance that God wants everyone in Christ to enjoy, or to the reality that they have not yet crossed from death to life and are in mortal peril.

It is one of the great myths of our time that it is unloving to tell people the truth of the gospel. My wife, Fiona, was recently speaking at a kids' ministry event and underlined the importance of laying the grand truths of the gospel—like God's grace and majesty and mercy and judgment—before children in ways that they can understand and embrace. In the Q&A session afterwards, one person said incredulously, "You aren't suggesting that we tell children about... HELL? That would be so unloving!" Well no, it wouldn't. Because real love gently but firmly tells the truth—love challenges.

7. Love prays

As he nears the end of his letter, Paul prays for the Corinthians, and he tells us exactly what he prays for them in the midst of this fraught situation: "But we pray to God that you may not do wrong ... that you may do what is right, though we may seem to have failed" (**v 7**). Ultimately, Paul doesn't really care about what they think of him; the main game is whether or not they repent and cling to Christ. That's what he prays for. If they do that, then they have nothing to fear from

Paul—as he says in **verse 8**, "For we cannot do anything against the truth, but only for the truth". If they have repented, then all is well. In fact, even if they still think Paul is a wimp, that's ok, because, for Paul, it really is all about them: "For we are glad when we are weak and you are strong. Your restoration is what we pray for" (**v 9**). This is what love looks like. This is what love prays for.

Paul longs for his visit to be a happy one because that means the Corinthians will have come back to the gospel and are living wholeheartedly for Christ. According to **verse 10**, he has written this letter to clear the way for a visit in which "I may not have to be severe in my use of the authority that the Lord has given me for building up and not for tearing down". He prays for God to work in their lives, enabling them to return to him in repentance and faith. He prays for them to embrace the gospel. That's what love does.

> Paul prays for them to embrace the gospel. That's what love does.

Love pursues, gives, builds, confronts, mourns, challenges and prays—and in particular, it prays for God to do his work in the lives of the people we love by enabling them to grasp and live out the gospel.

So what should we pray for those who persecute us? That God would deepen his work in their lives. What should we pray for those who don't rate us, or don't like us, or don't agree with us? That God would deepen his work in their lives. What should we pray for those who are closest to us? That God would deepen his work in their lives. For this is where love takes us. And with that, Paul draws this stunning letter to a close.

A surprising joy

It does come as a bit of a surprise when Paul signs off with the command in **verse 11**: "Finally, brothers, rejoice". But then, that has been his goal all along. That's why he adds, "Aim for restoration, comfort one another, agree with one another, live in peace". Taken together, these five simple statements sum up what he's been aiming for from chapter 1. He longs that they find joy in Christ and the relief that comes through repentance and forgiveness; that they encourage one another through the gospel and stand together for the gospel as they bask together in the peace of God, which is ours in and through the Lord Jesus. He longs for them to know that "the God of love and peace" is with them.

Can you feel the warmth? It's so obvious that Paul loves these men and women deeply—he loves them like Christ himself. This is such a moving conclusion. No wonder that he tells them to "greet one another with a holy kiss". This is a thoroughly Pauline expression of the purity and the unity—the close relationships, the family relationships—that the love of Christ creates both within local churches and even between local churches, as he passes on the greetings of "all the saints".

And then he concludes with the well-known words of **verse 14**, which underline that our God—Father, Son and Spirit both calls us to and equips us for the gospel-shaped life: "The grace of the Lord Jesus Christ and the love of God and the fellowship of the Holy Spirit be with you all". This is what the Corinthians needed. This is what Paul needed. This is what we need.

A final word from Baxter:

"Our whole work must be carried on under a deep sense of our own insufficiency, and of our entire dependence on Christ. We must go for light, and life, and strength to him who sends us on the work."   (*The Reformed Pastor,* p 62)

For as we have seen so often in this letter, when we are weak, then we are strong in Christ.

Questions for reflection

1. The love that God has shown us in Christ moves us to show the same kind of gospel-shaped concern for others. Do we care enough to mourn over the lack of growth in others? What can we do about our priorities?

2. For Paul, loving the Corinthians meant challenging them to be godly. How does this fit with our understanding of love? Why do we find it so hard to gently and lovingly confront others?

3. How does Paul's love for the Corinthians express itself in his prayers for them? What is the most loving thing we can pray for other people?

Questions for reflection on the whole book

1. Take a moment to write down three key things that God has taught you through 2 Corinthians.

2. Now write down three things that God has challenged you to do differently in the power which he supplies in Christ through the Spirit.

GLOSSARY

Agora: the market-place in a Roman city.

Alliterative: a list of words that start with the same letter, so that they are easier to remember.

Apostle: one of the men appointed directly by the risen Christ to teach about him with authority.

Augustine: a 4th-century bishop in north Africa. He taught that sin has entirely corrupted our human nature, and that we are powerless to overcome it, and so salvation is entirely God's gift and initiative.

Carnal: physical, especially sexual, needs and desires.

Charismatic: a kind of church that emphasises the gifts of the Holy Spirit.

Church discipline: how a church challenges and encourages those members who stray from faithful Christian living.

Claudius: Roman emperor AD 41 – 54

Commentary: a book that explains the meaning of a part of the Bible.

Condescend: to act in a way that shows you believe yourself to be superior.

Confession: in this context, a public acknowledgement that something is true.

Credobaptists: those who advocate baptism as an adult after a confession of faith.

Discipleship: following Jesus as Lord and trusting him as Saviour.

Doctrine: the study of what is true about God; or a statement about an aspect of that truth.

Edification: helping people grow in their Christian understanding and life through teaching them from the Bible.

Elders: those responsible for the teaching and ministry of a church.

Elitist: someone who thinks that society or a church should be led by those who are superior in intelligence or wealth.

Evangelicals/Evangelicalism: Christians and churches that emphasise the Bible's authority and the need to be personally converted through faith in Jesus' death and resurrection.

Evangelism: telling other people the *evangel*: the gospel message.

Evil one: the devil, Satan.

Excommunication: to exclude someone from the church, so that they are no longer recognised as a member of the church.

Exhortation: strong encouragement or urging to change or continue something.

Expository: teaching that explains the text of the Bible in detail.

Eye-service: doing what is expected only when people are looking.

Fallen: those who are affected by the fall—the event when the first man and woman disobeyed God (Genesis 3); sinful.

Gentiles: people who are not ethnically Jewish.

Gospel: the proclamation that the man Jesus was also God himself, who has come to serve us and to rule us as our King; that he died for sins; that he rose to rule and give new life; that he is reigning in heaven and will return to restore the world. The gospel is good news to be believed, not good advice to be followed.

Grace: unmerited favour. God's generous attitude towards people to forgive them and give them gifts.

Hellenistic: relating to ancient Greek culture.

Incarnation: the coming of the divine Son of God as a human in the person of Jesus Christ.

Intemperance: a lack of moderation or restraint.

INTJ, ESFP: different types of personality according to popular psychological tests.

John Bunyan: 17th-century English Puritan preacher who wrote *The Pilgrim's Progress*.

Journeymen: travelling workmen or artisans.

Judaisers: people within the early church who insisted that Christians should follow Jewish rules and rituals.

Julius Caesar: Roman emperor 49 – 44 BC.

Key signature: musical term; a metaphor for the guiding principle in someone's life.

Mediated, Mediator: someone who brings two enemies together and makes it possible for them to be friends again.

Messiah: Christ, the anointed one. In the Old Testament, God promised that the Messiah would come to rescue and rule his people.

Metaphorical: an image which is used to explain something, but which is not to be taken literally.

Ministry: the work of proclaiming the gospel in some way.

Misogynist: a woman-hater.

New creation: where God will gather all his people at the end, as described in Revelation 21 – 22.

Old/New covenant: The old covenant set out how believers in the Old Testament were to relate to God. Jesus established the new covenant, so believers now relate to God through his saving death and resurrection.

Orators: public speakers who were skilled in influencing people.

Orthodox: standard, accepted Christian teaching.

Overseer: a leader in the church or in a household.

Paedobaptists: those who advocate the baptism of children.

Parody: a mocking, exaggerated imitation of someone's ideas.

Piety: religious good deeds.

Propitiation: to turn away God's anger against sinners. Jesus' death on the cross is the way that God's anger at sinners is propitiated.

Prosperity gospel: a heresy stating that God promises to give material wealth to all his followers.

Public square: public conversation or debate.

Puritan: a member of a 16th- and 17th-century movement committed to the Bible as God's word, to simpler worship services, and to greater commitment and devotion to following Christ.

Reconciliation: when two hostile parties are brought together.

Redemption: when something is bought back at a price. This idea is used to describe how Jesus' death reconciles us to God.

Reformed, Reformation: someone who holds to the teaching of those who preached the gospel of justification by faith, and opposed the teaching of the Roman church in the 15th and 16th centuries.

Repentance: literally, a military word meaning "about turn." Used to mean turning around to live the opposite way to previously.

Rhetoric, Rhetorical: persuasive, manipulative speech. A **rhetorical question** does not expect to get an answer.

Righteousness: holy; the status of being in right relationship with God.

Saints: ordinary Christian believers.

Sealed with the Spirit: those who have received the Holy Spirit; Christians.

Shalom: Hebrew word for "peace".

Siege engine: an ancient military device for breaking city walls.

Sophists: philosophers who use clever words and ideas.

Tablets of stone: the stones that God wrote the ten commandments on, which Moses brought down from Mount Sinai.

Talents: a unit of weight and currency in the ancient world.

Theology/Theological: the study of or statements of the truth about God.

Titus: one of Paul's ministry partners. He spent time in Corinth, and acted took messages and news between the church there and Paul. Later, Paul wrote to him the letter we call "Titus", by which time Titus was one of the leaders of the church in Crete.

Universalist: someone who believes that everyone will be saved.

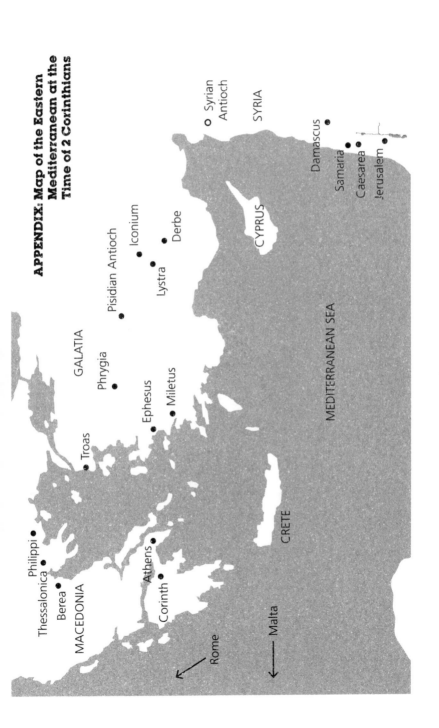

APPENDIX: Map of the Eastern Mediterranean at the Time of 2 Corinthians

MACEDONIA
Philippi
Thessalonica
Berea
Athens
Corinth
Troas
GALATIA
Phrygia
Ephesus
Miletus
Pisidian Antioch
Iconium
Lystra
Derbe
CYPRUS
Syrian Antioch
SYRIA
Damascus
Samaria
Caesarea
Jerusalem
CRETE
MEDITERRANEAN SEA
Rome
Malta

BIBLIOGRAPHY

Commentaries on 2 Corinthians

- Gerald Bray (ed), *2 Corinthians, Ancient Christian Commentary on Scripture* (IVP UK, 2006)

- C. K. Barrett, *2 Corinthians* (Baker, 1993)

- John Calvin, *Commentary on 2nd Corinthians* (Oliver & Boyd, 1964)

- D. A. Carson, *From Triumphalism to Maturity: 2 Corinthians 10 – 13* (IVP UK, 1986)

- David E. Garland, *2 Corinthians,* NAC (B&H, 1999)

- George H. Guthrie, *2nd Corinthians,* BECNT (Baker, 2015)

- Murray J. Harris, *The Second Epistle to the Corinthians*, NIGTC (Eerdmans, 2005)

- Matthew Henry, *An Exposition of Several Epistles contained in the New Testament* (1721)

- Charles Hodge, *I & II Corinthians* (Banner of Truth, 1974)

Other works referred to

- Christopher Ash, *Pure Joy: Rediscover your Conscience* (IVP UK, 2012)

- Herman Bavinck, *Reformed Dogmatics* (Baker, 2008)

- Richard Baxter, *The Reformed Pastor* (Edinburgh, 1989)

- John Bunyan, *The Pilgrim's Progress* (Penguin, 2009)

- James Denney, *The Christian Doctrine of Reconciliation* (Hodder & Stoughton, 1917)

▪ Jonathan Edwards, *The End for which God Created the World*, in John Piper, God's *Passion for His Glory* (Crossway, 1998)

▪ Thomas Goodwin, *The Works of Thomas Goodwin* (Banner of Truth, 1985)

▪ Nathaniel Hawthorne, *The Scarlet Letter* (Penguin, 2016)

▪ Richard Hooker, *A Learned Discourse of Justification, Works, and how the Foundation of Faith is Overthrown* (www.ccel.org/ccel/hooker/just.ii.html, accessed 25th October 2019)

▪ J. I. Packer, *Evangelism and the Sovereignty of God* (IVP UK, 1961)

▪ J. I. Packer, *A Passion for Holiness* (IVP UK, 1992)

▪ Blaise Pascal, *Pensées* (Penguin, 1995)

▪ John Piper, *Brothers, We Are Not Professionals* (B&H, 2013)

▪ John Piper, *Desiring God* (IVP UK, 1986)

▪ John Piper, *Future Grace* (Multnomah, 2005)

▪ John Piper, *The Supremacy of God in Preaching* (Baker, 1990)

▪ Bruce W. Winter, *Philo and Paul Among the Sophists* (Eerdmans, 2001)

2 Corinthians for...
Bible-study Groups

Gary Millar's **Good Book Guide** to 2 Corinthians is the companion to this resource, helping groups of Christians to explore, discuss and apply Paul's passionate and encouraging letter together. Seven studies—each including investigation, apply, getting personal, pray and explore more sections—take you through Paul's letter. Includes a concise Leader's Guide at the back.

Find out more at:
www.thegoodbook.com/goodbookguides

Daily Devotionals

Explore daily devotional helps you open up the Scriptures and will encourage and equip you in your walk with God. Available as a quarterly booklet, *Explore* is also available as an app, where you can download notes on 2 Corinthians and other books of the Bible, alongside contributions from trusted Bible teachers including Tim Keller, Stephen Um, Albert Mohler, Sam Allberry and Juan Sanchez.

Find out more at:
www.thegoodbook.com/explore

More For You

Romans 8-16 For You

"In Romans 8, you discover how to really use the gospel in
your heart to change in a profound way: and the rest of
the book will show you what that change will look like."

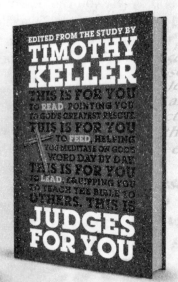

Judges For You

"Our era can be characterized by the phrase: 'Everyone did
as he saw fit' (Judges 21:25). So the book of Judges has
much to say to the individualism and paganism of our
own day. And it has much to say about the God of grace,
who works in the worst of situations, and who triumphs
over the stupidest of actions."

The Whole Series

Find out more about these resources at:
www.thegoodbook.com/for-you

Good Book Guides
for groups and individuals

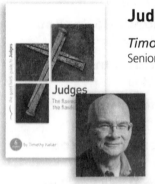

Judges: The flawed and the flawless

Timothy Keller
Senior Pastor, Redeemer Presbyterian Church, Manhattan

Welcome to a time when God's people were deeply flawed, often failing, and struggling to live in a world which worshipped other gods. Our world is not so different—we need Judges to equip us to live for God in our day, and remind us that he is a God of patience and mercy.
Also by Tim Keller: Romans 1–7; Romans 8–16; Galatians

Daniel: Staying strong in a hostile world

David Helm
Lead Pastor, Holy Trinity Church, Chicago

The first half of Daniel is well known and much loved. The second is little read and less understood! David Helm leads groups through the whole book, showing how the truths about God in the second half enabled Daniel and his friends—and will inspire us—to live faithful, courageous lives.

Esther: Royal rescue

Jane McNabb
Chair of the London Women's Convention

The experience of God's people in Esther's day helps us in those moments when we question God's sovereignty, his love, or his faithfulness. Their story reveals that despite appearances, God is in control, and he answers his people's prayers—often in most unexpected ways.

1 Corinthians 1–9: Challenging church

Mark Dever
Senior Pastor of Capitol Hill Baptist Church in Washington DC and President of 9Marks Ministries

The church in Corinth was full of life, and just as full of problems. As you read how Paul challenges these Christians, you'll see how you can contribute to your own church becoming truly shaped by the gospel.
Also by Mark Dever: 1 Corinthians 10–16

James: Genuine faith

Sam Allberry
Associate Minister, St Mary's Maidenhead, UK

Many Christians long for a deeper, more whole-hearted Christian life. But what does that look like? This deeply practical letter was written to show us, and will reveal how to experience joy in hardships, patience in suffering and whole-heartedness in how you speak, act and pray.
Also by Sam Allberry: Man of God; Biblical Manhood

1 Peter: Living well on the way home

Juan Sanchez
Preaching Pastor, High Pointe Baptist Church, Austin, Texas

The Christian life, lived well, is not easy—because we don't belong in this world. Learn from Peter how to journey on rather than retreat, and to do so with joy and hope, rather than gritted teeth.

COMPANY

BIBLICAL | RELEVANT | ACCESSIBLE

At The Good Book Company, we are dedicated to helping Christians and local churches grow. We believe that God's growth process always starts with hearing clearly what he has said to us through his timeless word—the Bible.

Ever since we opened our doors in 1991, we have been striving to produce Bible-based resources that bring glory to God. We have grown to become an international provider of user-friendly resources to the Christian community, with believers of all backgrounds and denominations using our books, Bible studies, devotionals, evangelistic resources, and DVD-based courses.

We want to equip ordinary Christians to live for Christ day by day, and churches to grow in their knowledge of God, their love for one another, and the effectiveness of their outreach.

Call us for a discussion of your needs or visit one of our local websites for more information on the resources and services we provide.

Your friends at The Good Book Company

thegoodbook.com | thegoodbook.co.uk
thegoodbook.com.au | thegoodbook.co.nz
thegoodbook.co.in